T0209345

Endorsements

In *The Testimony of Christ*, Steve Lange has written a straight forward, no sugar coating book that speaks God's truth from His word, *The Bible*. In it, Steve introduces the reader to Jesus, the Christ, who is the Lamb of God, slain from the foundation of the world. Steve discusses the testimony of Christ, the evidence that corroborates it, and the doctrine of Christ. Although it is not an exhaustive study, it clearly introduces the reader to Jesus, who He is, what He has done for all, and why one should believe Jesus is the Son of God. Throughout the book, Steve brings together threads of information from different places in *The Bible* and shows how God's story is woven throughout the book. Steve's research and presentation, with extensive references to *Bible* verses, provides the reader with a clear view of Jesus, and His love for us demonstrated by His willingness to die for our sins so that we might have eternal life. I highly recommend this book for those who are seeking the truth and those who are new believers.

Russ Harper, Systems Engineer,
Mt. Vernon, TX

Everyone has an opinion about Jesus. But not everyone has the time or the ability to sort through all the claims and evidence about him. Steve Lange helps us with this challenge by taking us step-by-step through statements of the many witnesses and the claims of Christ himself. Who is He, where did He come from, and why did He come? Does the evidence hold up under inspection? And what does it all mean to me?

Steve lays it all out in an interesting and compelling writing style, examining point after point, building a complete picture of the many claims of Jesus. Every page brings another thought provoking insight. The statements of various witnesses are brought together to support each point. The entire book is thoughtfully organized and easy to read.

For someone who is unsure about Jesus, this book clearly lays out the evidence and provides an opportunity to respond to the claims of Christ. For the Believer, this book is a refreshing opportunity to gain a deeper understanding of Jesus and strengthen their faith based on a careful examination of the evidence.

Steve Kirtley, New Victory Studios,
Knoxville, TN

Jesus Christ was the Messiah of God promised from ancient times to come and rescue and adopt those who believe and accept him and to redeem all of creation from the fall from Eden and to re-unite man and God (and heaven and earth). *The Testimony of Christ* is a through and systematic review of essentially every scripture regarding God's purpose and plan in sending Jesus to us to achieve that rescue. It is a direct, hard hitting, easy to read and unapologetic presentation of those Biblical statements, and it leads the reader to a clear conclusion of how we should respond to God's plan for our lives.

It is a must read for anyone who wonders what the Judeo-Christian western tradition is "all about" and why "those Christians" have had such a remarkable effect on the history of the western world for the last 2000 years, and it is also a must read for those nascent Christians, who are uncertain about what they need to do next, now that they have accepted Christ as their savior.

John C. Lange, M.D., Orthopaedic Surgeon, Redding, CA

Most people have heard of the central figure of all human history, Jesus. Most people have an opinion about him. But who is he, really? That's what this book answers. Christology is a fancy term that theologians use to describe the study and doctrine of Jesus the Christ. Most of us don't have the time or the inclination to be full blown theologians. However, all of us, believer and unbeliever alike, owe it to ourselves to have a better understanding of who Jesus is.

The Testimony of Christ is the book for the rest of us. While the nature of the material is serious and complex, Steve pulls away the confusion and mystery in a book that is intuitively organized, and enjoyable to read.

Who will enjoy reading *The Testimony of Christ*? First, the unbeliever, the skeptic, and the seeker will all be gently challenged to learn about and perhaps come to meet an appealing Jesus they never knew. And also the believer, whether young or old in their faith, will learn surprising things that will draw them nearer to the Lord they love.

David Peterson, Senior Fellow
at The Center for the Study of The Great Ideas
San Jose, CA

The Testimony of Christ

STEPHEN W. LANGE

WESTBOW
P R E S S®
A DIVISION OF THOMAS NELSON
& ZONDERVAN

WestBow Press books may be ordered through booksellers or by contacting:

WestBow Press
A Division of Thomas Nelson & Zondervan
1663 Liberty Drive
Bloomington, IN 47403
www.westbowpress.com
1 (866) 928-1240

Cover Design by Rob Williams, Designer, *www.ilovemycover.com*

ISBN: 978-1-9736-4296-1 (sc)
ISBN: 978-1-9736-4297-8 (e)

Print information available on the last page.

WestBow Press rev. date: 11/13/2018

Author's note: Modern *Bible* translations are copyrighted works and limit
the number of verses that can be quoted in a book like this. The *King James
Version* (KJV) of *The Bible* is in the public domain and has no restrictions
on the number of verses that can be quoted. Most of the quoted *Bible*
verses in this book are from the KJV to ensure that no copyright limits are
exceeded. In some cases, a more modern translation is quoted for clarity.

Contents

1 Introduction

I grew up hiking, backpacking, and camping in the mountains with my family. As an adult, I continued hiking and backpacking, and I took motorcycle camping trips all over the Sierra Nevadas and the Rocky Mountains. There was something about being in the mountains that spoke to me, the grandeur and scale of them, and the beauty and diversity of life.

My dad always told me that random evolutionary processes created everything that exists, but it seemed hard to believe that we were here by accident. I kept looking at the world around me and thinking that there must be a God. Everything around us and we ourselves couldn't be here by chance could we? What purpose is there in our lives? Is there a reason why we're here? Do our lives matter?

When I was eighteen I had a girlfriend that was a Christian, and one day I attended a Billy Graham crusade with her and went down to the altar and I asked God to forgive me and save me. But I didn't feel any different. Had I really spoken to God? Had He heard me?

I started looking around at other religions and investigating them. I told myself that I was seeking God, and different religions just had different ways of finding Him. Did every religion lead to God? Why were they different if we were seeking the same God? Were they different solely because of different cultures? Do all religions have the truth about God?

1

I had a friend who was very involved in Yoga and I started hanging out with him, practicing Yoga, and reading all of the books on it I could find. I was exercising and meditating, searching for God. I was groping in the dark looking for God and hearing many voices, each of them telling me to follow them. Everyone was saying something different. Deep in my heart I knew that God existed. How could I find God? How could I tell which way to go? How could I know the truth?

The longer I went without finding an answer to my questions, the more they receded into the past. I became just someone living however I wanted without very much thought about God at all, thinking I would learn the truth when I died.

But after a number of years, God drew me back to *The Bible*. The truth dawned on me. God had been calling me my whole life, but I hadn't been listening. But, God is gracious and never stops calling us to come to Him.

To everyone who sincerely comes to God and asks for understanding, God promises to reveal Himself to them. God wants us to know Him, and has made a way for us to do that.

2 How Can We Know the Truth?

One day I was standing on the public sidewalk outside of a high school in Boca Raton, Florida with a group of Gideons, handing out New Testaments to the students as they left campus. A Jewish mother of one of the students came up to us incensed that we were offering New Testaments to the students. I talked with her for a few minutes, and as she was leaving, she told me that Christians were worshipping an idol. Ever since that conversation a few years ago, I've been thinking about what she said. Was she correct when she said that Jesus is an idol Christians worship? Many people around the world would agree with her. They say that Jesus is just a man, and it is wrong to worship him. I wanted to tell her how we could know who Jesus is.

The four Gospels[1] record many things that Jesus said, including definitive statements that He made about himself. There are many people that deny the claims of Christ and say that the Christian church has made up many of the characteristics of Christ long after He lived on the earth. They claim that the four Gospels are an apocryphal account of His life, and they don't really tell the truth about Christ. This has led to different movements in liberal theology where people claim to be searching for the historical Jesus. They ignore the testimony of eyewitnesses to His

---

[1] The books of *Matthew, Mark, Luke,* and *John* in the *New Testament.*

life recorded in *The Bible*, and then search for the truth of Christ while denying *The Bible*.

Opponents of Christ and Christianity claim that the church made up the doctrine of the deity of Christ after His death. They claim that the Trinity of God was also made up after the fact. They claim that people edited the Gospels and Epistles of the New Testament written by the apostles and disciples long after their deaths and they are unreliable. Are the four Gospel accounts of Jesus Christ apocryphal or are they a truthful record of the person, life, and work of Christ? Are the images and ideas that we have of Christ and the doctrines that are at the foundation of the Christian church correct? Is there a way to corroborate the testimony of Christ as given in the four Gospels?

Why is it important to know the truth of these matters? The biblical account of Christ and Christianity directly contradicts the testimony of every other religion. They cannot all be true because they contradict each other. If one is true the others are false. How do we know which account of God is true?

The Buddhists claim that God is unknowable and not a person. *The Bible* claims that a personal God created man in the likeness of God, giving him intelligence, morality, and will,[2] and that not only is God knowable, but God wants man to know Him.[3] Islam claims that Jesus is a prophet of God, but that He didn't die on the cross for the sins of the world. Islam claims that God has no Son. Yet *The Bible* says that God testified to the fact that Jesus is His Son by His death and resurrection.[4] The Mormons and Jehovah's Witnesses claim that Jesus is a created being and not God. *The Bible* claims that Jesus is God and uncreated.[5] Judaism claims that Jesus is not the Messiah. *The Bible* claims that Jesus is

---

[2] Genesis 1:26.
[3] Jeremiah 31:34; Hosea 6:6.
[4] Acts 17:30-31; Romans 1:1-4.
[5] John 1:1-3, 1:14, 8:58.

the Messiah.[6] The secular world says that there is no God. Yet *The Bible* calls men fools for not believing in God.[7]

Should we believe the Biblical account of Jesus Christ and reject what the world and other religions say about Jesus? How can we know the truth? In order to ensure that the conclusions that we draw from the testimony of Christ are correct, we have to know if *The Bible* reliably records what Jesus said and did.

The first premise of all non-believers is that God doesn't exist, any supernatural acts are impossible, and therefore any document that reports miracles or supernatural acts is obviously untrue. They reject the witness of *The Bible* and then search for evidence of who and what Jesus is.

Secular sources acknowledge that Jesus lived and traveled around Galilee and Judea in the early years of the first century AD when Pontius Pilate was the Roman governor of Judea. Other than accounts of Jesus' baptism and His crucifixion under the rule of Pontius Pilate by Josephus and Tacitus, there is no other documentary evidence of Jesus outside of *The Bible*.

The only writings quoting what Jesus said are found in the Gospels, the Acts of the Apostles, and in the epistles of the New Testament. Early church leaders quoted all these sources in their letters to each other. So if one rejects the testimony of *The Bible*, then there is nothing to go on to decide what Christ said or didn't say.

Unbelievers reject the truth of *The Bible*, but not because there is not evidence for it. There is abundant evidence that *The Bible* is true. But people willingly ignore that evidence because it contradicts their hope and belief in naturalism, the idea that everything that exists came about by random natural processes.

This book is not going to make an argument about the

---

[6] Acts 2:36.
[7] Psalms 14:1-3.

reliability of the Biblical record, other than to affirm that it is a reliable record of what Jesus said and did.

For people interested in the evidence that *The Bible* is a reliable record, please consult any or all of the sources listed in the Appendix at the end of this book. All of the cited sources testify to the reliability of our *Bible*. We can trust that it is a faithful translation of the original documents written by eyewitnesses to the life, teachings, death, and resurrection of Christ.

So what is the testimony of Jesus Christ that the eyewitnesses report? Jesus Christ claimed to speak the truth about God and himself. Jesus said that we could know whether his claims are true. What evidence did Jesus claim to corroborate his testimony? We will be investigating the testimony of Christ and the corroboration that Jesus claimed for showing it to be true.

We can know for sure whether the testimony of Christ as recorded in *The Bible* is true. We only need to honestly examine the evidence given to us by Christ.

3 What Say You of Christ?

Jesus asked the Pharisees, the Jewish religious leaders, who the Christ, the Messiah, is:

> *While the Pharisees were gathered together, Jesus asked them, saying, "What do you think about the Christ? Whose Son is He?"* (Matthew 22:41-42 NKJV)

The Pharisees replied that the Messiah would be the son of David. Jesus asked them why, if the Messiah is David's son, David himself, moved by the Holy Spirit, calls him Lord?[8] The fact that David called the Messiah Lord says that he is more than David's son.

Another time, Jesus asked His disciples who men thought he was:

> *When Jesus came into the region of Caesarea Philippi, He asked His disciples, saying, "Who do men say that I, the Son of Man, am?"* (Matthew 16:13 NKJV)

People had various opinions about Jesus. Some thought he was Elijah come back to the earth. The Old Testament reports that

---

[8] Matthew 22:43-45.

Elijah had been taken to heaven alive,[9] and so people thought he had returned in fulfillment of prophecy.[10] Or, they thought that Jesus was John the Baptist resurrected, or that he was one of the other prophets.

Jesus asked the apostles who they thought He was:

> *Simon Peter answered and said, "You are the Christ, the Son of the living God."* (Matthew 16:16 NKJV)

The Greek name translated Jesus in our English *Bible* is "Iesous"[11] from the Hebrew name Jehoshua or Joshua, and means, "Jehovah is Salvation" or "Jehovah Saves." We usually refer to Jesus as Jesus Christ, but the name "Christ" is a title. Jesus refers to himself as "the Christ", or in some translations, "the Messiah."[12] The name Christ is translated from the Greek word "Cristos," and is the Greek translation of the Hebrew word, "masiyah," i.e., Messiah, meaning "Anointed One."

We have to ask ourselves, "Who is Jesus?" Was Jesus just a good man, maybe a better man than most who have lived, or was he something else?

What was Jesus' purpose in his ministry? Was Jesus trying to teach people how to be good? Will God accept us if we're good? How good do we have to be for God to accept us?

Why was Jesus crucified? Was Jesus resurrected from the dead? Did the followers of Jesus decide on their own to found a religion in his name? Is Christianity just a man-made religion? Did Jesus claim to be God? Or, did his followers make him God after his death on the cross?

When people say that there is no God, they answer each of these questions from the premise that only the natural world

---

[9] 2 Kings 2:11.

[10] Malachi 4:5.

[11] Strong's number g2424 from Luke 1:31, from h3091, 'Yhwh-saved', i.e., Joshua.

[12] Matthew 16:20 NLT.

exists, and there is a natural explanation to answer every question. They gloss over the one fact that they know is true that refutes their belief in naturalism, and that is the creation of the universe out of nothing, at a moment in time, contrary to the laws of physics.[13] All energy, matter, time, and the laws of physics that describe their interaction came into existence at the same time as the universe itself, so something outside of the universe had to have created it.

There is a God who created the universe, but people close their eyes to that fact and they ignore Him. The creation of the universe shows that there is a God.[14] He is a God powerful enough to create the universe. He is a God wise and intelligent enough to specify how it functions in every detail. The creation has testified to everyone that God exists. But the creation only verifies His existence, it doesn't say who God is. It tells us very little about what He thinks or if we can know Him.

How can we know the truth about God? Is the God of *The Bible* the God who created the universe and everything in it? Is Jesus the only witness to God as *The Bible* claims?

"What do you think about the Christ, whose Son is He?"

---

[13] *I Don't Have Enough Faith to Be an Atheist – Chapter 3*, by Normal L. Geisler and Frank Turek. Copyright © 2004. Published by Crossway Books, a division of Good News Publishers, 1300 Crescent Street, Wheaton, Illinois 60187.
[14] Psalms 19:1-3; Romans 1:19-20.

4 The Testimony of Christt

What testimony did Jesus give while on the earth? Jesus spoke concerning who God is, who He is, where He came from, why He came, what He was doing, and why He was doing it. He witnessed to what was going to happen in the future. He testified to the fact that there is a God in heaven and that we will all have an existence after death.

People in opposition to Jesus Christ believe His statements in *The Bible* were probably made up after the fact of his life and death. The miracles and statements reported of Jesus are obviously impossible, and therefore cannot be true.

In order to know the truth we must know what Jesus Christ gave witness to.

4.1 Jesus Is God

Many unbelieving biblical scholars and apologists for other religions state that Christians turned Jesus into God after the fact. They claim that the early Christian church retroactively claimed the deity of Jesus after His crucifixion in order to bolster the claims of Christianity on the lives of people. They don't believe the eyewitness testimony of the resurrection of Christ. If we search on the phrase "The Historical Jesus"[15] in Wikipedia we find the following claims by some New Testament scholars.

Raymond E. Brown states that early Christians did not call Jesus God:

> *There is no reason to think that Jesus was called God in the earliest layers of New Testament tradition.*[16]

John Hick states that Jesus didn't think of himself as God or make any claims to that effect:

> *A further point of broad agreement among New Testament scholars ... is that the historical Jesus did not make the claim to deity that later Christian thought was to make for him: he did not understand himself to be God, or God the Son, incarnate. ... such evidence as there is has led the historians of the era to conclude, with an impressive degree of unanimity, that Jesus did not claim to be God incarnate.*[17]

Did the early Christians call Jesus God? Seeing Jesus in the flesh after his resurrection confirmed His deity to the apostles. Upon hearing of the resurrection from the other apostles Thomas said he would refuse to believe unless he saw the resurrected Christ for himself:

> *...Except I shall see in his hands the print of the nails, and put my finger into the print of the nails,*

---

[15] *https://en.wikipedia.org/wiki/Historical_Jesus*

[16] "Does the New Testament call Jesus God?" by Raymond E. Brown in Theological Studies, 26, (1965) p. 545-73.

[17] "The Metaphor of God Incarnate" by John Hick. Copyright ã 1993,2005. Westminster John Knox Press. Page 27.

and thrust my hand into his side, I will not believe.
(John 20:25 KJV)

Thomas was with the other apostles when the resurrected Jesus appeared to them a second time. Jesus told Thomas to look at him and examine him and see that it was Jesus Christ himself, he really had come back from the dead. When Thomas saw Jesus alive, he confessed, "*My Lord and my God.*"[18] The Apostle Thomas confessed that Jesus Christ was God.

So, contrary to Raymond Brown's statement, the early Christians did call Jesus God. They didn't adopt the idea fifty or a hundred years later. They called Jesus God immediately after His resurrection and before His ascension to heaven.

Paul, in his letter to the Romans, called Jesus, "*God blessed forever,*" when he was speaking about Israel and the fact that Jesus Christ came through the bloodline of the Jews.[19] Paul claims the same thing in his letter to Titus, that Jesus is God.[20] Paul's letter to the Romans was written sometime between 55 and 60 AD,[21] and the letter to Titus in approximately 66 or 67 AD.[22] So again, it has been shown that the early Christians considered Jesus God.

What did Jesus Himself testify concerning these issues? John Hick claims that Jesus didn't think of Himself as God or ever claim to be God. Is this true? Did Jesus think of Himself as God? Did Jesus ever claim to be God?

The Gospel of Mark records an instance of Jesus and the disciples walking through a field of grain and the disciples plucking the grain, rubbing it in their hands to remove the husk or chaff and eating it.[23] The Pharisees accused the disciples of doing

---

[18] John 20:28 KJV.
[19] Romans 9:3-5 KJV.
[20] Titus 2:13.
[21] *https://en.wikipedia.org/wiki/Epistle_to_the_Romans*
[22] *https://en.wikipedia.org/wiki/Epistle_to_Titus*
[23] Mark 2:23-28.

something that was not lawful to do on the Sabbath, because it was work. Jesus' response to the Pharisees was that He is *"Lord of the Sabbath."* By claiming to be Lord of the Sabbath, Jesus was claiming to be God. Looking back at the *Ten Commandments* that God gave Israel, the fourth commandment is, *"Remember the Sabbath day, to keep it holy."*[24] God clarifies His instructions about the Sabbath, and calls it, *"the Sabbath of the Lord thy God."* The same event is reported in Luke.[25] Both Mark and Luke state that Jesus claimed to be Lord of the Sabbath. Jesus testified that He is Lord of something that only God is Lord of.

Jesus told the Jews that He was greater than the prophet Jonah and wiser than King Solomon:

> *The men of Nineveh shall rise in judgment with this generation, and shall condemn it: because they repented at the preaching of Jonas; and, behold, a greater than Jonas is here. The queen of the south shall rise up in the judgment with this generation, and shall condemn it: for she came from the uttermost parts of the earth to hear the wisdom of Solomon; and, behold, a greater than Solomon is here.* (Matthew 12:41-42 KJV)

Not only did Jesus testify that He was greater than the prophet Jonah and wiser than Solomon, but when testifying to His being Lord of the Sabbath, Jesus told the Jews that He was greater even than the temple:

But I say unto you, that in this place is one greater than the temple. But if ye had known what this meaneth, I will have mercy, and not sacrifice, ye would not have condemned the guiltless. For the Son of man is Lord even of the Sabbath day. (Matthew 12:6-8 KJV)

---

[24] Exodus 20:8-11 KJV.
[25] Luke 6:1-5.

The entire city of Ninevah in Assyria humbled themselves before God, sitting in sackcloth and ashes, at the preaching of Jonah. They confessed their sin, turned from their evil ways, and asked God to forgive them.[26] Jesus stood before the Jews, testifying that He was God Almighty, greater than everyone who had come before Him, and called on them to repent and believe the gospel.[27]

Jesus stated that He has the power to forgive sins.[28] One day He was teaching in a house, and the house was completely full. Four men who had faith that Jesus could heal their paralytic friend tried to enter the house to get to Jesus and they couldn't. So, they climbed up on the roof and breaking through the roof, lowered their friend down in front of Jesus, who told the paralytic, *"Son, thy sins be forgiven thee."* The scribes and Pharisees hearing Jesus say that the man's sins were forgiven thought within their hearts, *"Why doth this man thus speak blasphemies? Who can forgive sins but God?"*

Not only was Jesus claiming to be God because He could forgive sin, but Jesus demonstrated that He is God by revealing what they were thinking in their hearts. Jesus declared to them plainly that His healing of the man was proof that He had the power to forgive sins. The relating of the healing of the lame man and forgiving his sins is found in all three of the synoptic Gospels.[29] This wasn't the only time that Jesus exercised His authority as God to forgive people of sins. He absolved the woman who washed his feet with her hair and her tears of her sins when dining with the Pharisees.[30] Jesus claimed to be God with authority to forgive sins and then acted as God in forgiving people of their sins.

At another time, Jesus told the Pharisees that if anyone kept His word, they would never die, claiming that He has the power

---

[26] Jonah 3:5-10.
[27] Mark 1:14-15.
[28] Mark 2:1-12 KJV.
[29] Matthew 9:2-6; Mark 2:1-12; Luke 5:17-26.
[30] Luke 7:48-50.

that only God has, to keep people from dying.[31] The Pharisees asked Him if He were greater than Abraham, who was dead. Jesus told the Pharisees that He had existed from before Abraham, *"Before Abraham was, I AM."* It wasn't just that Jesus claimed to be older than Abraham. Jesus was claiming to have existed eternally.

At the burning bush when God called Moses to lead Israel in the Exodus from Egypt, Moses asked God to tell him His name.[32] God told Moses to tell Israel *"I AM has sent me to you."* God referred to Himself as, *"I AM,"* meaning He exists. Later God tells Moses that His name is "YHWH,"[33] translated as "LORD" (all capitals) by the English *Bible* translators and pronounced as "Yahweh," or in some translations, "JHVH," "Jehovah," which is a Latinized spelling of "YHWH." The name, "Yahweh," or "Jehovah" means, "The Self-Existent or Eternal."[34] When Jesus told the Pharisees, *"I AM,"* He was claiming to be God, and they knew it. They immediately took up stones to kill Him for blasphemy.

This isn't the only time that Jesus claimed that He had existed forever. When praying to God for the disciples at the last supper Jesus acknowledged that He had been with God from before the creation of the world.[35] Jesus explicitly stated that He had been in glory with God the Father from antiquity. The claim of Jesus is not just that He has existed forever. The claim of Jesus is that He is the eternally self-existent, uncreated, God.

Jesus told the disciples that He and God were one and the same, *"I and my Father are one."*[36] Jesus told His disciples that they could know that He and God were one by the miracles that He performed.[37] Jesus told His disciples that when they believed in

---

[31] John 8:48-59 NKJV.
[32] Exodus 3:14 NKJV.
[33] Exodus 6:2-3.
[34] Strong's number h3068 'yhwh' from Exodus 6:3.
[35] John 17:4-5.
[36] John 10:30.
[37] John 10:37-38.

Him they were really believing in God, and when the disciples saw Him they were seeing God.[38] At the Last Supper, His apostle Phillip asked Him to show them God, and Jesus claimed His own deity when he told them, *"He that hath seen me hath seen the Father."*[39] Jesus stated explicitly that whoever sees Him sees God and whoever knows Him knows God.

Jesus implicitly stated that He is God by receiving the worship of men. In the *Ten Commandments* it states that no one other than God is to be worshipped, and when speaking of idols says, *"you shall not bow down nor worship them."*[40] When Jesus was tempted by Satan to fall down and worship him, Jesus rebuked him saying, *"Thou shalt worship the Lord thy God, and him only shalt thou serve."*[41]

The Roman Centurian, Cornelius, had seen an angel in a vision who told him to call for the Apostle Peter, who would come and tell him what to do. When Peter arrived, Cornelius fell down before him to worship him. Peter refused the worship of Cornelius, stating that he is a man just as Cornelius.[42]

In the book of Revelation, the Apostle John was overcome by the glory of what had been revealed to him by the angel. He fell down before the angel to worship. But the angel rebuked him and told him to worship God alone.[43]

People were always rebuked when they tried to worship men or angels, but Jesus accepted the worship of men without rebuking them. He was acknowledging that it was proper to worship Him because he is God.

The leper came and fell down before Jesus and worshipped Him, and asked Jesus to heal him. Jesus touched the man and

---

[38] John 12:44-45.
[39] John 14:7-11.
[40] Deuteronomy 5:6-9.
[41] Luke 4:7-8 KJV.
[42] Acts 10:25-26.
[43] Revelation 22:8-9.

healed him of his leprosy.[44] In the Old Testament, if someone had leprosy they were not to touch others or allow others to touch them. They were to live away from other people and whenever they came close to other people they had to cry out, *"Unclean, unclean."*[45] Jesus was not only willing to cleanse and heal him, but He touched him, something no one had done since the man had contracted leprosy. Jesus accepted the worship of the leper.

Jairus, the ruler of the synagogue, had a daughter who had died, and he was looking to Jesus to bring her back from the dead. When he came to Jesus, he fell down and worshipped Him. He told Him that even though his daughter was dead, Jesus could bring her back to life by laying His hands on her.[46] Luke confirms that he fell down at Jesus feet.[47] Jesus accepted the worship of Jairus.

Jesus had sent the disciples ahead of Him across the sea. A storm had come up and the disciples were fighting against the wind and the waves. Jesus came to them walking on the water. He called Peter out of the boat to come to Him and Peter walked on the water until he took his eyes off of Jesus and instead fixed them on the storm. Jesus rescued him from drowning and they both entered the boat. As soon as Jesus and Peter entered the boat, the storm died. The disciples worshipped Jesus as God and Jesus accepted their worship.[48]

When Jesus traveled to the region of Gadarene, a man who was possessed of evil spirits met him. Seeing Jesus he ran to Him and worshipped Him; *"But when he saw Jesus afar off, he ran and worshipped him."*[49] Not only did Jesus accept the worship of the man, but also He commanded the unclean spirits to depart from him, demonstrating His power over spirits.

---

[44] Matthew 8:2-3.
[45] Leviticus 13:45 KJV.
[46] Matthew 9:18.
[47] Luke 8:41.
[48] Matthew 14:31-33.
[49] Mark 5:6 KJV.

Jesus healed a man who had been born blind. Afterwards, when the man claimed that it was Jesus who healed him, the Pharisees told the man that they didn't know whether Jesus was really from God. The man was astonished at their stubborness. Because he testified to the Pharisees that Jesus was obviously from God, they excommunicated him from the temple. Later, Jesus found the man and testified to him that He is the Son of God, and the man worshipped Him.[50]

Finally, the women at the tomb worshipped Jesus as God upon his resurrection. The angels at the tomb had told them to go and tell the apostles of His resurrection and Jesus met them on the way. They ran to Him and fell at his feet and worshipped Him.[51]

Jesus testified that He is Lord of the Sabbath. Jesus testified that He is wiser than Solomon and greater than the temple in Jerusalem. Jesus stated that He had the power and authority to forgive sins. Jesus demonstrated that He knew what men were thinking. Jesus claimed that He had power over life and death. Jesus told people that He was uncreated and had existed forever. Jesus said that when people saw Him, they saw God and that anyone that knows Him, knows God. Jesus implied that He is God by receiving the worship of men, something *The Bible* forbids for anyone other than God. Jesus spoke in authority over spirits.

Jesus thought of Himself as God. Jesus claimed to be God. Jesus acted as God. The testimony of Jesus Christ is that He is God. The early church was just reporting what they had been eyewitnesses to:

> *But Peter and John answered and said unto them, whether it be right in the sight of God to hearken unto you more than unto God, judge ye. For we cannot*

[50] John 9:30-38.
[51] Matthew 28:9.

> *but speak the things which we have seen and heard.*
> (Acts 4:19-20 KJV)

4.2 Jesus is the Son of God

From our earlier search in Wikipedia on "The Historical Jesus", Gerd Lüdemann states that the early Christian church made up Jesus' exalted nature:

> *"The broad consensus of modern New Testament scholars that the proclamation of Jesus' exalted nature was in large measure the creation of the earliest Christian communities".* [52]

Did the early Christians make up Jesus' exalted status as the divine Son of God, the Messiah?

On Palm Sunday, the week before the crucifixion of Jesus, when He entered the city of Jerusalem riding a donkey, His disciples following Him were crying out, *"Blessed is the King who comes in the name of the Lord."*[53] Jesus was already exalted in their eyes. They didn't wait until later to make up His exalted status. They proclaimed Him as the Messiah, the King of Israel, even before His death.

Peter preached to the Israelites on the day of Pentecost, fifty days after the Passover, the day when Christ was crucified. Peter told them that Jesus was the Messiah spoken of by David in Psalm 16 and promised to Israel in the Old Testament. They had crucified their Messiah, but God had raised Him from the dead, and Peter and the apostles had witnessed His resurrection.[54] The day of Pentecost was only a couple months after the death and

---

[52] "An Embarrassing Misrepresentation" by Gerd Lüdemann. Free Inquiry, Oct/Nov 2007.

[53] Luke 19:37-38 KJV.

[54] Acts 2:30-32,36.

resurrection of Christ. Peter proclaimed Jesus' exalted status almost immediately; he didn't make it up.

Later when preaching to the gentiles in Cornelius' home, Peter said that they were eyewitnesses to everything that Jesus did: the miracles and healings while He was alive, and the resurrection of Jesus after His death. Peter stated that they ate and drank with Him after His resurrection.[55] The apostles proclaimed that Jesus was the fulfillment of prophecy of all of the prophets in the Old Testament who spoke of the Messiah. God exalted Jesus in front of the apostles and the disciples by His resurrection from the dead. They testified to that fact, saying that Jesus had commanded them to tell everyone that He had been anointed and exalted by God, and made judge of both the living and the dead.

Jesus himself told the disciples who followed Him, the crowds that He taught, the Pharisees, the priests, and the scribes that He is the Son of God.

As the Son of God, Jesus healed a man who had been lame for thirty-eight years, lying beside the pool at Bethesda waiting for healing. When the Pharisees accused Jesus of breaking the Sabbath by healing the man, Jesus replied that God was His Father and since the Father is working, Jesus is working. The Pharisees knew that when Jesus was claiming to be the Son of God, He was claiming equality with God.[56]

The previous section referring to Jesus accepting the worship of men recounted the story of the man born blind that Jesus healed.[57] The man worshipped Jesus when Jesus testified to him that He is the Son of God. His healing corroborated the testimony of Christ.

At the illegal trial before the Sanhedrin on the night before he was crucified, the High Priest, Caiaphas, asked Jesus directly if

---

[55] Acts 10:38-43.
[56] John 5:17-18.
[57] John 9:30-38.

He were the Christ, the Son of God, and Jesus affirmed that He was. The exchange between Jesus and the high priest is told in all three synoptic Gospels.[58] In the account in Matthew, the high priest confirms that the Messiah and the Son of God are one and the same person. And Jesus then tells the High Priest that He will see the Son of Man sitting at the right hand of the throne of God. Jesus refers the High Priest directly to the prophecy of the Messiah where God says to the Messiah, *"Sit thou at my right hand, until I make thine enemies thy footstool."*[59] Not only that, but Jesus uses the terms Christ, Son of God, and Son of Man interchangeably. In Luke 22 Jesus refers to Himself as the Son of Man, and the members of the Sanhedrin understood that He was saying that He is the Son of God. The Christ, the Son of God, and the Son of Man are all the same person, and Jesus testified that it is He.

When the rulers and chief priests asked Pilate to condemn Jesus, the reason they gave is that Jesus claimed to be the Son of God.[60] Jesus testified that He is the Son of God and everyone, even His enemies, knew that He had testified to that. The church didn't make up the exalted status of Jesus. Jesus proclaimed it, and the apostles and disciples believed it and reported it.

4.3 Jesus is the Messiah

When Jesus started his ministry he entered into the synagogue in Nazareth and proclaimed Himself to be the Messiah. He read a prophecy of the Messiah from the book of Isaiah[61] and stated that the passage had its fulfillment in Him.[62] God had prophesied that He would anoint the Messiah to preach the gospel to the poor, to heal those who were broken hearted, to preach deliverance to

---

[58] Matthew 26:63-64; Mark 14:61-62; Luke 22:69-70.
[59] Psalms 110:1 KJV.
[60] John 19:7.
[61] Isaiah 61:1-2a.
[62] Luke 4:16-21.

all of those held captive, to heal the blind, and to preach that the kingdom of God was now at hand. Jesus testified to those in the synagogue, telling them:

> ... *"Today this Scripture is fulfilled in your hearing."*
> (Luke 4:21b NKJV)

Notice that by saying that the passage had its fulfillment in Him, Jesus was testifying that He was the one God had anointed, the Messiah. The Psalmist refers to God's Son as *"his anointed"*,[63] the Messiah.

When Jesus was speaking with the woman of Samaria at the well, He told her that God is Spirit and He was looking for true worshippers, for people to worship Him in spirit and in truth. The woman replied that when the Messiah comes he would reveal everything to them. Jesus told the woman that He is the Messiah, the one who was prophesied to come.[64]

At the start of his ministry Jesus openly said that He was the Christ. However, after the people had rejected Him and accused Him of being in league with Beelzebub,[65] another name for Satan, He hid that knowledge from the crowd. When Jesus questioned His disciples about who people said He was, Simon Peter confessed Jesus as the Christ, but Jesus warned them not to make that known.[66]

He knew that if He openly testified that He was the Christ, the people would try to proclaim Him King of Israel in fulfillment of the prophecies that the Messiah would be the king. When the people saw the miracle of the feeding of the 5,000, they said that surely Jesus was the Prophet spoken of by Moses,[67] i.e., the Messiah.

---

[63] Psalm 2:2 KJV. Strong's number h4899, 'masiyah', anointed, i.e., the Messiah.
[64] John 4:23-26.
[65] Luke 11:15.
[66] Matthew 16:15-16,20.
[67] Deuteronomy 18:15-19.

Jesus had to depart from them to ensure they didn't try to come and make Him king by force.[68] The two different views of the Messiah in the Old Testament, one a sacrifice for sin[69] and the other a reigning king[70] confused people, so they ignored the image of the suffering Messiah, and instead focused on the Messiah as the reigning king.

Just as Jesus explicitly testified that He is the Son of God. Jesus explicitly testified that He is the Christ, the Messiah promised to Israel.

4.4 Jesus is Lord and King

The disciples and crowds following Jesus called Him Lord. Jesus rebuked them for acknowledging that He is Lord but refusing to do what He said. He promised that everyone who acknowledged that He was Lord and obeyed what He said would have their lives blessed. Anyone who refused to acknowledge Him as Lord and heed His words would have their lives cursed.[71]

It wasn't just that other people called Jesus Lord. Jesus Himself acknowledged that He is Lord. When teaching the apostles on the night before his crucifixion, Jesus explicitly stated that He is their Lord.[72] Later that same night, Jesus testifies that God has given Him authority over life and death, making Him Lord of all creation.[73] As Lord over life and death Jesus Christ has the power and authority to give eternal life to whom He chooses but sentence others to eternal destruction.

The rulers of Israel knew that Jesus' claim to be Lord and Messiah meant that He was also claiming to be King of the Jews.

---

[68] John 6:14-15.
[69] Isaiah 53.
[70] Psalms 2, 45, 110; Daniel 7.
[71] Luke 6:46-49.
[72] John 13:13.
[73] John 17:1-3.

Since the prophecies of the Messiah in the Old Testament proclaim Him as the king who would rule all of creation,[74] the rulers used this to accuse Jesus in His trial before Pontius Pilate, saying that He was a king in rebellion against Caesar.[75] Pilate questioned Jesus about whether this was true, and Jesus acknowledged that it was; He is the King of the Jews.[76] The rulers and chief priests told Pilate that if he didn't execute someone claiming to be a king, he was no friend of Caesar. This accusation was the one that forced Pilate to crucify Jesus.[77]

When Pilate had Jesus crucified he wrote an inscription that they nailed to the cross over Jesus, *"The King Of The Jews."*[78] The priests and Pharisees denied Jesus' testimony that He is the King of the Jews and asked Pilate to change the inscription to show that instead of Jesus being King of the Jews, Jesus only claimed to be King of the Jews.[79] Pilate rebuked them and let stand the title of Jesus on the cross as *"The King Of The Jews."* Even the enemies of Jesus acknowledged that as the Messiah He claimed to be the King of the Jews.

On the day before Jesus was crucified, He promised His disciples that He would return with the holy angels as the king of all creation and sit on the throne of His glory. He testified that as the king, He would judge the nations and separate them into two groups, the righteous on His right hand and the wicked on His left. He will cast the wicked on His left hand into the everlasting fire, but the righteous on His right hand will enter into the kingdom of God.[80]

The apostles and disciples understood that Jesus claimed to

---

[74] Psalms 2, 110; Daniel 7, et al.
[75] Luke 23:2.
[76] Matthew 27:11.
[77] John 19:12.
[78] Luke 23:38 KJV.
[79] John 19:21-22.
[80] Matthew 25:31-46.

be the king promised to Israel. Before His ascension up to heaven, knowing Him to be the king, they asked Him if He was going to restore the kingdom to Israel at that time.[81] Jesus told them not to worry about the timing of when He would return to take up His reign, which was known to God the Father alone.

4.5 Jesus Came From Heaven

Jesus specifically testified to people that He had come from God in heaven to the earth. He told Nicodemus, a ruler of the Jews, that He had come down from heaven. No man living had ever seen heaven except the Son of Man who came from heaven.[82] When Jesus speaks of the Son of Man, He is referring to Himself. Jesus came from heaven to testify concerning God. No one living knows about heaven because no one has been there. Only Christ who came from heaven can testify to the facts of God and heaven.

Later Jesus explicitly testified to His disciples and the Pharisees and priests following him that He came from heaven above:

> And He said to them, "You are from beneath; I am from above. You are of this world; I am not of this world. (John 8:23 NKJV)

He told the Pharisees that if they loved God they would love Jesus because He had come from God in heaven. Not only did He come from God, but also God specifically sent Him.[83]

Jesus was claiming deity when He said, "*I and my Father are one.*"[84] The Jews took up stones to kill Jesus and He asked them why they wanted to kill Him. They replied that they were going to stone Him because He was making Himself God. Jesus replied

---

[81] Acts 1:6-7.
[82] John 3:11-13.
[83] John 8:42.
[84] John 10:30 KJV.

that He had been sanctified, and sent by God into the world.[85] He was telling them the truth; He had come from God.

4.6 Jesus is the Witness to God

Jesus testified that He is from God, and He has seen God the Father.[86] No one else has ever seen God the Father except Jesus. Jesus testified that people came to Him because God sent them so that they could know God.[87] No one other than Jesus had ever seen God, so no one other than Jesus could ever reveal who God is to people. Even Moses was not allowed to see God. Moses asked God to let him see Him, and God replied, *"Thou canst not see my face: for there shall no man see me, and live."*[88] For no man shall see God and live. Jesus' testimony that He has seen God is an implicit claim to deity. He is the only one who has seen God and lived.

Jesus testified to people that He is the only witness to God, the only one who knows who God is. Jesus stated that no one is able to know God unless Jesus reveals God to him or her.[89]

In support of His role as the witness of God the Father, Jesus testified that God gave the very words that He spoke to Him.[90] He said nothing on His own:

> *I have many things to say and to judge of you: but he that sent me is true; and I speak to the world those things which I have heard of him. They understood not that he spake to them of the Father. Then said Jesus unto them, When ye have lifted up the Son of man, then shall ye know that I am he, and that I do*

---

[85] John 10:32-33,36.
[86] John 3:11,13, 6:46.
[87] John 6:44-45.
[88] Exodus 33:19-20 KJV.
[89] Luke 10:22.
[90] John 14:10, 17:8.

> *nothing of myself; but as my Father hath taught me,*
> *I speak these things.* (John 8:26-28 KJV)

4.7 Jesus Came To Save Mankind

In many statements that Jesus made, He plainly stated why He had come. He told everyone what His mission and His purpose were in coming. He left no one in doubt of where He had come from and why He was there.

He prefaced His statements by telling everyone that He was there in the authority of God the Father, He was there in the name of God. He reprimanded the Pharisees for not believing Him, and said it was because they didn't have the love of God in them. They rejected Jesus and the authority of God resting on Him.[91]

Not only did Jesus come in the name of God, but also He came to carry out God's will.[92] Jesus was so burdened to carry out the will of God that He told His disciples that carrying out God's will was food to His soul.[93] Jesus testified that being obedient to the will of God was more important than His life. He acknowledged this before God the Father in the Garden of Gethsemane prior to His arrest.[94] He then acknowledged the same thing in front of His own disciples. When the priests and Pharisees sent men to arrest Jesus in the garden, His disciples wanted to fight to protect Him. Jesus told Peter to put away his sword because His arrest was according to the will of God, and He was acting in obedience to God's will.[95]

Later, when Jesus was standing before Pilate, He told him that if His kingdom were from this world, His followers would fight to keep Him from falling into the hands of the Jews. Jesus was

---

[91] John 5:42-43.
[92] John 6:38.
[93] John 4:34.
[94] Matthew 26:39,42.
[95] John 18:10-11.

following the will of God by submitting to the authority of Pilate.[96] Jesus told Pilate that Pilate's authority came from God,[97] so when Jesus submitted to Pilate, he was submitting to God.

As an aside, a parallel to this was when Jesus told the Pharisees, *"Render therefore unto Caesar the things which be Caesar's, and unto God the things which be God's."*[98] Since everything Caesar had really belonged to God, giving Caesar what was his was really giving God what belonged to Him. God is the owner of everything by right of creation.[99] In the same way, Jesus was acknowledging that all authority flows from God.

When Jesus stated that He always did those things that pleased God,[100] He was stating that He was always obedient to God's will. Jesus perfectly kept God's will; He was perfectly obedient to him. God's will was always that people would obey His word. Yet throughout the history of man on earth, no one except Jesus has ever perfectly carried out God's will. Jesus testified that as part of following God's will He came to fulfill God's law.[101]

Man had refused to carry out the will of God in obedience to His word. Instead, every man had gone his own way, ignoring God. Jesus came to call people to repentance, to acknowledge that they had sinned before God, and to return to Him. When He started his ministry He called on people to repent and believe the Gospel.[102] Jesus testified that one of the reasons why He came was to call people to repentance, to call them to turn back from following their own will, and turn towards God and His will.[103] Jesus confirmed that no one had kept the will of God when

---

[96] John 18:36.
[97] John 19:10-11.
[98] Luke 20:25 KJV.
[99] Psalms 89:11.
[100] John 8:29.
[101] Matthew 5:17-18.
[102] Mark 1:14-15.
[103] Luke 5:31-32.

He stated that there was no one good but God.[104] God in his righteousness declared death to be the penalty for sin.[105] All sin is rebellion against the will and word of God.[106]

Jesus told Nicodemus that He had come to save the world from the penalty of their sin. Everyone had sinned, the penalty for sin is death, and so everyone was under sentence of death. Jesus testified that God sent Him into the world to save it so that people wouldn't perish under the judgment of God.[107] Jesus' disciples wanted to destroy the people in a village that had rejected Christ. Jesus told his disciples that He had come to save men's lives, not destroy them.[108]

Jesus testified how He was going to save the world. He was going to give His own life as a ransom for the people who were under the wrath of God because of sin.[109] Jesus came to pay the penalty for sin that God's righteousness demanded. Jesus testified that His blood is the blood of the new covenant, which would be shed for the remission of sins.[110] It is the blood of Jesus sealing the promise of God to forgive people because of the death of Christ on their behalf, and make a way for them to be reconciled to God.

4.8 Jesus Would Die and Be Resurrected

There were two separate episodes in the Biblical account where Jesus entered the temple and cleansed it of people buying and selling sacrificial animals and changing money in the area that God had meant for prayer. The first time was at the start of His

---

[104] Mark 10:18.
[105] Ezekiel 18:4.
[106] 1 John 3:4.
[107] John 3:16-18.
[108] Luke 9:54-56.
[109] Matthew 20:28; Mark 10:45; John 10:15.
[110] Matthew 26:28.

ministry and is described in the Gospel of John.[111] The second time was at the end of his ministry after He entered Jerusalem on Palm Sunday, the week of His crucifixion.[112] In the account of the cleansing at the start of His ministry, the Jews asked Jesus to show them a sign proving to them that He had the authority to command what activity was allowed in the temple. Jesus replied that if they destroyed the temple, He would rebuild it in three days. The Jews thought Jesus was referring to the temple of Herod, but John tells us that Jesus was referring to His own body. If they killed Him, He would be resurrected after three days.

Later in His ministry, the Jews came to Jesus asking for a sign to prove that He is the Messiah. They had already seen many miracles of Jesus, but they wanted another sign. Jesus told them that the only sign that would be given them would be the sign of the prophet Jonah.[113] He had already told them that just as Jonah was three days and three nights in the belly of the fish or whale [KJV], so the Son of Man would be three days and three nights in the heart of the earth.[114] Jesus stated that He would lie in the tomb dead for three days and three nights and be resurrected. The death and resurrection of Jesus is the one sign from God given to all people of the truth of Christ.

When Jesus was speaking with Nicodemus he told him that just as Moses lifted up the serpent in the wilderness, the Son of Man must be lifted up so that whoever believes in Him will not perish.[115] The serpent that Jesus is referring to is the bronze serpent that God told Moses to make.[116] The people had been murmuring and complaining about Moses and God and had aroused God's anger, and *The Bible* says that He sent fiery serpents that bit the

---

[111] John 2:12-22.
[112] Matthew 21:12-13.
[113] Matthew 16:4.
[114] Matthew 12:40.
[115] John 3:14-15.
[116] Numbers 21:5-9.

people and they died. The people confessed to Moses that they had sinned, and God told Moses to make a bronze serpent and lift it up on a pole. Whenever anyone was bitten, they were to look at the serpent on the pole in faith to God, and they would live. Jesus was prophesying of His death on the cross and telling Nicodemus that whoever looked to Jesus would be saved.

Jesus told people that He was going voluntarily to His death.[117] When Peter confessed that Jesus was the Messiah, Jesus told the apostles that He was going to build His church on Peter's confession. The church of Christ would be built on the confession of Peter to the truth that Jesus is the Messiah who would die to pay for the sins of people. Right after Christ reveals that He is going to build His church, He tells the disciples that He is going to suffer many things from the chief priests and elders of Jerusalem and die, but He would be raised again on the third day.[118]

Jesus reiterated to His disciples over and over that He was going to Jerusalem to die at the hands of the leaders of Israel. He would die, but He would rise again the third day.[119] The disciples understood that Jesus had testified that He was going to die. When Jesus told them that they needed to go to Bethany so He could resurrect Lazarus, Thomas told the other disciples that they should go and die with Him.[120] What the disciples failed to understand was Jesus' statement that He was going to rise again.

The rulers of the Jews knew that Jesus had testified that He would be resurrected. At his trial they tried to use His quote that he would rebuild the temple in three days as an indictment against him.[121] When Jesus was crucified and hanging on the cross, they laughed at Him, reviled Him, and dared Him to come down from

---

[117] John 10:17-18.
[118] Matthew 16:16-21.
[119] Matthew 17:22-23, 20:17-19; Mark 9:9-10.
[120] John 11:15-16.
[121] Matthew 26:61.

the cross in fulfillment of His claim to be the Messiah, the King of the Jews, and His statement to rebuild the temple in three days.[122]

They knew that Jesus had claimed that He would be resurrected. They proved their knowledge of His testimony concerning His resurrection when they went to Pilate and asked him to set a guard around the tomb to stop the disciples from claiming the resurrection in fulfillment of His prophecy.[123] If the body of Christ had remained in the tomb, then a guard would have refuted any claims to a resurrection.

Matthew tells us that Jesus was resurrected, and an angel from heaven rolled back the stone from the tomb. The soldiers guarding the tomb were struck down in fear upon seeing this.[124] The angel didn't roll the stone back to allow Jesus to come out. He rolled the stone back to allow the disciples to enter in and witness that Jesus had been raised from the dead.[125]

When Jesus appeared to the apostles and disciples who were locked in the upper room for fear of the Jews, He showed them proof of His physical resurrection. He told them that it was He Himself, and not a spirit. He told them to touch Him and see that He had flesh and bones[126]. He asked them to give Him something to eat, and He ate a broiled fish and a honeycomb before them. He was physically resurrected from the dead in fulfillment of His testimony.

Jesus promised people that His death and resurrection would be the only sign that would be given to them to let them know the truth of what He said.[127] Jesus also testified that because of His resurrection, repentance and forgiveness of sins would be proclaimed in His name to all nations.[128]

---

122 Matthew 27:39-42.
123 Matthew 27:62-66.
124 Matthew 28:2-6.
125 Luke 24:2-8; John 20:5-8, 11-12.
126 Luke 24:36-43; John 20:19-20.
127 Luke 11:29-32.
128 Luke 24:46-47.

5 Corroborating the Testimony of Christ

J esus testified that the word of God is the truth when He was praying for the apostles. He prayed to God the Father that God would sanctify or separate the apostles from the world by the truth of God, which is His word.[129] He didn't pray only for the apostles to be sanctified by the truth of God's word; He prayed for all those who would come to believe in Christ because of the word of God preached by the apostles.[130]

Jesus claimed that just as the word of God is the truth, His testimony is true. The Old Testament specified that you needed at least two witnesses to anything to ensure its veracity.[131] The Pharisees called Jesus a liar because He was witnessing to Himself without a corroborating second witness.[132] Jesus acknowledged the truth of the Scriptures, and agreed that He was testifying to Himself. But He claimed that God the Father was testifying to the same thing, making two witnesses to the truth. The miracles that He did were the witness from God to the truth of what Jesus testified. The verification of His truthfulness was the fact He is never alone, God is always with Him, and God is bearing witness to the truth of Christ.[133] He told the Pharisees that if they had

---

[129] John 17:17.
[130] John 17:20.
[131] Deuteronomy 19:15.
[132] John 8:13.
[133] John 8:14-19.

known Him they would have known the Father, but that they knew neither Him nor the Father. Jesus continually testified that He is God by saying that if the Pharisees knew Him they would know God. A little later in the conversation with the Pharisees, Jesus reiterates that God the Father is always with Him because He always does those things that please God.[134] Jesus claimed that His testimony is the truth, and God the Father corroborated it.

Jesus stated that He only spoke what God commanded Him to speak. Jesus said nothing on His own. Every single statement of Jesus was in obedience to God the Father and to the purpose of God for sending Christ to the earth.[135] Not only is Jesus saying that He's speaking only what God told Him to speak, but He's making an implicit claim to sinlessness, to perfection.[136] He never misspoke, He never lied, and He never spoke any evil.

Jesus testified that the doctrine that He revealed was not His but God's.[137] Every lesson He taught to the apostles, to the disciples, to the people He healed, and to the Pharisees and religious leaders, was from God. Jesus was the witness to the truth of God. When Pilate asked him if He were a king, Jesus replied that He was, and the reason that He had come into the world was to testify to the truth.[138] Jesus told Pilate that everyone who is of the truth hears His voice.

When Jesus testified that He bore witness to the truth of God, the Pharisees withstood Him. Jesus told the Pharisees that they couldn't understand His words because they weren't of God; they were of their father, the devil.[139] Jesus called on them to convict Him of sin and they couldn't.

Jesus testified that the words of His witness would never pass

---

[134] John 8:29.
[135] John 12:49-50.
[136] James 3:2.
[137] John 7:16-17.
[138] John 18:37.
[139] John 8:42-47.

away. The earth and the heavens would pass away, but the words that Jesus spoke from God would remain.[140] Jesus promised that the very words of His witness would be what judged people at the end.[141] Whoever rejected His testimony would be condemned.

Jesus claimed there is corroboration for the truth of His testimony, and He tells us that the corroboration comes from four witnesses:

> *You have sent to John, and he has borne witness to the truth. Yet I do not receive testimony from man, but I say these things that you may be saved. He was the burning and shining lamp, and you were willing for a time to rejoice in his light. But I have a greater witness than John's; for the works which the Father has given Me to finish – the very works that I do – bear witness of Me, that the Father has sent Me. And the Father Himself, who sent Me, has testified of Me. You have neither heard His voice at any time, nor seen His form. But you do not have His word abiding in you, because whom He sent, Him you do not believe. You search the Scriptures, for in them you think you have eternal life; and these are they which testify of Me.* (John 5:33-39 NKJV)

The four witnesses that corroborate the testimony of Christ are:

- John the Baptist
- The works (miracles) that He did
- God the Father
- The Scriptures (i.e., the Old Testament)

---

[140] Matthew 24:35.
[141] John 12:48-50.

Jesus showed us where to investigate to corroborate His testimony.

5.1 The Corroboration of John the Baptist

Jesus claimed that John the Baptist corroborated His testimony. Who was John the Baptist? Upon a cursory examination of the Gospels he seems to play a very minor role. How significant is John the Baptist? What does *The Bible* say about him?

John the Baptist was the son of Zacharias and Elizabeth, both of whom were of the tribe of Levi and descendants of Aaron. Zacharias was a member of the Levitical priesthood of Israel and Elizabeth was the daughter of a Levitical priest. They had no children and were both now old.[142] When, as priest, it was Zacharias' turn to burn incense in the temple, he went in and the angel Gabriel appeared to him. Gabriel told him that they were going to have a son, whom they would name John. Gabriel told Zacharias that his son would be filled with the Holy Spirit from birth and he would be a forerunner of the Messiah, the Christ, calling people to repentance.[143]

John the Baptist's mother, Elizabeth, was the cousin of Mary, the mother of Christ. Luke tells us that when Elizabeth was six months pregnant with John, the angel Gabriel appeared to Mary and told her that she was going to give birth to Jesus.[144] Mary became pregnant with Jesus by the Holy Spirit and went to stay with her cousin, Elizabeth. At the moment she entered the house, Elizabeth (and John in her womb) were filled with the Holy Spirit and she prophesied over Mary and acknowledged that the baby Mary was carrying was the Lord.[145]

The Bible says nothing about the life of John the Baptist as

---

[142] Luke 1:5-7.

[143] Luke 1:13-17.

[144] Luke 1:26-38.

[145] Luke 1:39-45.

a child. The next reference to him is when *The Bible* says that the word of the Lord comes to him during the rule of Annas and Caiaphas, the high priests. John was living in the wilderness and he started preaching a baptism of repentance for the remission of sins.[146]

The apostle John tells us that John the Baptist was sent by God to bear witness to the light of Christ.[147] John said that the reason he came baptizing people was so that Christ could be revealed.[148] John the Baptist had been sent to prepare the way beforehand for Jesus.[149]

In the book of Daniel, Daniel receives the vision of the seventy weeks of years, the times determined for Israel.[150] The prophecy says that from the time the decree goes out to rebuild Jerusalem after the return of the Jews from Babylon, to the time that the Messiah comes will be sixty-nine weeks of years, or 483 years. In his book, *The Coming Prince*,[151] Sir Robert Anderson lays out the calculations for the date of the proclamation to rebuild Jerusalem and its walls and of the Messiah being cut off in Jerusalem. Artaxerxes[152] decreed that Nehemiah would rebuild the walls of Jerusalem. This decree occurs in approximately 449 BC. Sir Robert Anderson shows that 483 years after the proclamation to rebuild Jerusalem, Jesus rides into Jerusalem on a donkey on Palm Sunday of the week of His crucifixion in approximately 33 AD, in accordance with Daniel's prophecy.

The priests and the members of the Sanhedrin, the ruling council of the Jews, knew the time that the Messiah was predicted to come from the prophecy of Daniel and this is the reason they

---

[146] Luke 3:3-4.
[147] John 1:6-8, 8:12.
[148] John 1:31.
[149] John 3:28.
[150] Daniel 9:24-27.
[151] *The Coming Prince* by Sir Robert Anderson, ~1892.
[152] Nehemiah 2.

questioned John The Baptist. They wanted to know if he was the Messiah, and John told them he was not the Messiah.[153] When they asked John to tell them who he was, he quoted from the Old Testament and said he was the voice of one crying in the wilderness to make straight the paths of the Lord.[154] Everyone was reasoning in their hearts whether John the Baptist was the Messiah prophesied to come. They knew from Daniel's prophecy that the time for the Messiah to appear was imminent. John told them that he was not the Messiah. The Messiah was already among them, but they didn't know him. He told them that he baptized with water, but the Christ would baptize people with the Holy Spirit and with fire.[155]

Jesus rebuked the Pharisees over the witness of John the Baptist.[156] John the Baptist was living in the desert eating only locusts and honey, dressed in camel hair.[157] He was living as an ascetic. The Pharisees refused the call of John the Baptist to repent and be baptized, trusting in their own self-righteousness, thinking they had nothing they needed to repent of.[158] They accused John the Baptist of having been demon possessed. The Pharisees had to deflect John's accusations of iniquity away from themselves.[159]

Jesus confirmed that John was the messenger sent before Christ, and Jesus Himself is the messenger of the covenant.[160] The people knew the scriptures but were blind to their meaning. The Lord, Jesus Christ, the Messiah, was standing before them.

Jesus testified that John the Baptist was the greatest prophet that had been born up until that point. Jesus said that all the

---

[153] John 1:19-23.
[154] Isaiah 40:3.
[155] Luke 3:15-16.
[156] Luke 7:31-35.
[157] Matthew 3:4.
[158] Luke 7:30.
[159] Matthew 3:7.
[160] Matthew 11:10; Malachi 3:1 KJV.

prophets and the law prophesied up until the point of John the Baptist, implying that there was an end to the law and the prophets.[161] Jesus would be the one to replace the covenant of the law with the new covenant of grace. Jesus said that John the Baptist was fulfilling the role of the prophet Elijah who was prophesied to appear before the coming of the Messiah.[162]

The Pharisees asked Jesus by what authority He was teaching the people, and Jesus replied that if they could tell Him by what authority John baptized people in repentance of sin, Jesus would tell them by what authority He taught. The Pharisees and Sadducees refused to answer because whichever way they answered would have revealed their duplicity.[163]

Jesus told the Pharisees:

> *You have sent to John, and he has borne witness to the truth.* (John 5:33 NKJV)

What truth was Jesus referring to? John said:

> *This was He of whom I said, 'He who comes after me is preferred before me, for He was before me.'* (John 1:15 NKJV)

Jesus said, "*Before Abraham was, I AM.*"[164] Jesus was born six months after John,[165] yet John testifies that Jesus came before him. John is corroborating Jesus' testimony that He has existed eternally.

John the Baptist reported that Jesus came from God, spoke

---

[161] Matthew 11:12-14.
[162] Malachi 4:5-6.
[163] Luke 20:1-8.
[164] John 8:58 NKJV.
[165] Luke 1:36.

the words of God, and had God the Holy Spirit indwelling Him, corroborating Jesus' testimony:

> For he whom God hath sent speaketh the words of God: for God giveth not the Spirit by measure unto him. (John 3:34 KJV)

When Jesus came to John to be baptized, John didn't want to do it, because he knew that Christ was sinless, and he was sinful. He told Christ that he was the one who needed to be baptized by Christ, not the other way around.[166] Jesus told him that it was fitting that John baptized Jesus because Jesus was fulfilling all righteousness by submitting to the baptism of John. It goes back to the reason that Jesus told people that He came, to fulfill the law and the will of God.

John tells us that Jesus is the Lamb of God who comes to take away the sins of the world.[167] John the Baptist confirmed Jesus' mission to redeem the world by giving His life as a ransom for all men. Calling Jesus the Lamb of God is a direct reference to the call of God to Abraham to sacrifice his son, Isaac.[168] Abraham told his son that God would provide the lamb for the sacrifice for sin. John telling his disciples that Jesus is the Lamb of God is confirmation that God has provided the sacrifice for sin that he promised to Israel. The Psalmist says that God forgives the iniquity of His people; He covers their sin.[169] God explicitly said that He was going to make the Messiah a sacrifice for sin. God promised Israel that He was going to provide an atonement for their sin, a fountain to cleanse them of their uncleanness.[170]

In the Old Testament, on the Day of Atonement, the High

---

[166] Matthew 3:13-15.

[167] John 1:29.

[168] Genesis 22:7-8,13.

[169] Psalms 85:2.

[170] Isaiah 53:10-11; Ezekiel 16:63; Zechariah 13:1.

Priest would enter into the Holy of Holies, where the Ark of the Covenant stood. On top of the Ark of the Covenant was the mercy seat, and over that the two Cherubim.[171] Inside the Ark of the Covenant, also called the Ark of the Testimony, were three items: the jar of manna, Aaron's rod that budded, and the tablets of stone containing the *Ten Commandments*. The Ark of the Covenant contained the testimony that man had rejected God and gone his own way. The Ark of the Testimony was a witness to man's sin and rebellion against God. The jar of manna signified that man had rejected God's provision.[172] Aaron's rod, a symbol of his office as the High Priest chosen by God, signified that man had rejected God's spiritual leadership.[173] The tablets of the *Ten Commandments* signified that man had rejected God's law.[174]

The Ark of the Testimony contained the proof of the guilt of mankind. Mankind deserved judgment. When the High Priest entered into the Holy of Holies on the Day of Atonement, he would sprinkle the blood of the sacrificial lamb on the mercy seat.[175] The blood of the sacrifice covered the sin of Israel. Jesus was the sacrificial lamb provided by God to cover the sins of mankind, signifying that blood had been shed in atonement for sin.

John gave witness that God identified Jesus as the Christ to him. God spoke to John the Baptist and told him that on whomever he saw the Holy Spirit descend was the Messiah, the one who baptizes with the Holy Spirit. John the Baptist testified that Jesus is the Messiah, the Son of God.[176] In the act of baptizing Jesus, John the Baptist received confirmation from God that Jesus is the Christ.[177]

---

[171] Hebrews 9:2-5.
[172] Numbers 11:4-6.
[173] Numbers 16:3,12-14.
[174] Deuteronomy 9:10-17.
[175] Leviticus 16.
[176] John 1:32-34.
[177] Matthew 3:17; Mark 1:11; Luke 3:22.

John the Baptist testified that Jesus is the bridegroom.[178] In the Old Testament, God told Israel that He was their husband, but they had rejected Him.[179] But God gave a prophecy of the betrothal of the Messiah, whom God called God.[180] When John the Baptist calls Jesus the bridegroom, it is a direct reference to the prophecies. Jesus refers to Himself as the bridegroom witnessed to by these scriptures. When answering an objection of the Pharisees about why His disciples don't fast, He tells them that there is no reason for them to fast when the bridegroom is with them. Jesus said the day would come when the bridegroom would be taken away and then His disciples would fast.[181] The issue wasn't if or when the disciples would fast; it was that Jesus is the bridegroom.

John the Baptist corroborated the testimony of Christ. He confirmed the eternal existence of Jesus. He testified to the truth that Jesus is the Messiah. He confirmed that Jesus spoke the words of God. He told his disciples that Jesus is the Lamb of God who takes away the sin of the world. And he witnessed to the fact that Jesus is the bridegroom spoken of in the prophecies of the Messiah. The people who followed John and had heard his witness to Christ believed and followed Jesus:

> Then many came to Him and said, "John performed no sign, but all the things that John spoke about this Man were true." (John 10:41 NKJV)

5.2 The Corroboration of the Miracles

The second witness corroborating the testimony of Christ are the very miracles that he performed. Jesus said:

---

[178] John 3:28-29.
[179] Isaiah 54:5; Jeremiah 3:20, 31:32.
[180] Psalms 45.
[181] Mark 2:18-20.

> But I have a greater witness than John's; for the works
> which the Father has given Me to finish – the very
> works that I do – bear witness of Me, that the Father
> has sent Me. (John 5:36 NKJV)

There were two reasons for the miracles of Jesus. One reason was that Jesus performed miracles out of compassion for people who were sick, in poverty, and had been oppressed by Satan. He healed people,[182] He fed people,[183] He cast out demons who oppressed them,[184] and He forgave them.[185]

The second reason for the miracles was to corroborate the truth of His testimony.[186] Every miracle of Jesus exhibited His love and compassion for people and was a witness to the truth of what He said.

Jesus commanded His disciples to love each other in the same way that He had loved them.[187] He laid down His life to prove His love.[188] Jesus is not just God claiming authority and ownership of everything and everyone, He is the one who proved His love by dying on the cross.

The miracles say that Jesus is the Christ, and that He came from God and spoke for Him. In addition, they were the fulfillment of prophecies in the Old Testament concerning the Messiah. Jesus said that God the Father who is in Him works the miracles. People can trust that what He said is true because of the miracles.[189]

---

[182] Matthew 14:14; Mark 1:41; John 5:6-9.
[183] Matthew 15:32-38; John 6:10-13.
[184] Matthew 17:14-18; Mark 1:34, 16:9; Luke 8:27-36.
[185] Matthew 18:27; Luke 23:34; John 8:3-11.
[186] John 10:37-38.
[187] John 13:34.
[188] John 15:13.
[189] John 14:10-11.

5.2.1 Miraculous Confirmation That Jesus is God

The miracles of Jesus confirm that he is God. As the creator of the universe and all life, God has power over His creation. When Jesus performed miracles, He exercised the power of God over His creation in a number of ways. His miracles showed that He ruled over the elements of the earth, the wind, and the seas. He miraculously made provision for people. His miracles of healing and resurrection proved that He was the author of life,[190] and controlled every aspect of it. He healed people as only their creator could, making them well and whole. He called people back from the dead. His miracles demonstrated his authority over the living and the dead whether man or spirit.

Jesus demonstrated his control over the physical elements of the world when He changed the water into wine at the wedding in Cana.[191] He was attending the wedding with his mother and his disciples. When the wedding feast ran out of wine, Jesus' mother told Jesus that they had no more wine and she told the servants to do whatever Jesus told them. He had the servants fill six large water pots full to the brim with water. He then told the servant to draw out some of the water and take it to the governor of the feast. The governor confirmed that the water had been made into wine when he praised the bridegroom for saving the best wine for last. The servants of the feast who drew the water knew that somehow Jesus had turned the water into wine. Jesus used the miracle of converting the water into wine to corroborate the truth of what He said to his disciples and they believed on Him.

One day after preaching to a multitude, Jesus and the disciples got into a boat to cross over to the other side of the Sea of Galilee.[192] Others boats were following the boat Jesus and the disciples were in. Jesus was tired and fell asleep in the boat and a great storm

---

[190] Acts 3:14-15 ESV.

[191] John 2:6-11.

[192] Mark 4:36-41.

arose creating large waves that were in danger of swamping the boats. The disciples woke Jesus up and asked Him if he cared whether they perished or not? Jesus rebuked the wind and the storm, saying, *"Peace, be still,"* and the sea was immediately calm; all of the boats were now safe. Jesus told His disciples that their fear came from a lack of faith:

> *And he said unto them, why are ye so fearful? How*
> *is it that ye have no faith?* (Mark 4:40 KJV)

Jesus used the miracle of the calming of the storm to show that, as God, He rules over the elements. He showed His disciples that they could safely trust in Him. Not only was the miracle of the calming of the storm confirmation that Jesus is God, but the miracle was a fulfillment of God's promise to answer sailors' prayers during a storm.[193]

A second time Jesus demonstrated that He is God with power over the elements was when He came walking on the sea to the disciples in the midst of a storm.[194] The disciples thought they were seeing a spirit and Jesus called out to them to not be afraid. Peter asked Jesus to prove that it was He by calling him to come out of the boat to Him, and Jesus said, *"Come."* Peter climbed out of the boat and was walking toward Jesus, but the wind and the waves distracted his attention away from Jesus and he began to sink. Peter called out, *"Lord, save me,"* and Jesus took him by the hand and led him back to the boat. When they entered the boat, the wind ceased. Jesus asked Peter why he had so little faith, why did he doubt? Seeing the miracle of Jesus walking on the water, of Peter walking on the water to him, and then the storm ceasing when they got into the boat led the other disciples to worship Jesus as the

---

193 Psalms 107:23-30.
194 Matthew 14:26-33.

Son of God. Jesus used the miracles to corroborate His testimony that He is the Christ to his disciples.

Jesus demonstrated that He is the God who provides for the people He created when He fed the multitudes. On two different occasions Jesus turned a small amount of food suitable for a few people into a feast for thousands. The feeding of the five thousand men, who could have been a crowd of fifteen or twenty thousand counting women and children, is the only miracle that is recorded in all four Gospels.[195] The second occurrence of Christ miraculously providing for people is told in the story of the feeding of four thousand men.[196] Again, the crowd was probably ten or fifteen thousand strong if women and children are counted. When questioned about the feeding of the five thousand, Jesus told the disciples that He was the bread of life that came down from heaven:

> For the bread of God is He who comes down from heaven and gives life to the world." ... And Jesus said to them, "I am the bread of life. He who comes to Me shall never hunger, and he who believes in Me shall never thirst." (John 6:33,35 NKJV)

The miracle was in support of Jesus' claim that He came from heaven.

In the Sermon on the Mount, Jesus told the disciples to not worry about having food to eat or clothes to wear. God the Father knows that they need these things, and He promises to provide everything they need, if they'll just put Him first.[197] Jesus told people if God cared and provided for the lowly creatures of the field, how much more would He provide for them? Jesus' two separate miracles of the feeding of large multitudes corroborate His

---

[195] Matthew 14:15-21; Mark 6:35-44; Luke 9:12-17; John 6:5-13.
[196] Matthew 15:32-38; Mark 8:1-9.
[197] Matthew 6:25-33.

testimony that not only does God care for His people and promise to provide for them, but He has the power to carry out His promise. His miracles prove that Jesus is God.

Jesus used his miracles of healing and the resurrection of the dead to corroborate His testimony that as God, He is the author of life, and Lord over all of creation.[198] In the Old Testament, the magicians of Pharaoh were able to copy some of Moses miracles but not all of them.[199] In the time of the tribulation, it says that Satan empowers the Antichrist and the False Prophet to perform miracles to deceive the people on the earth.[200] But the resurrection of the dead is the one miracle that only God can perform. As the author of life, Jesus calls the dead to life, and no one else has that power.

One day a leper came to Jesus and fell down and worshipped before Him and told Jesus that if He wanted He could make him clean.[201] Jesus healed the man to show that He is God, to show that the leper had been correct in falling down to worship Him. But more than that, Jesus showed the man that the heart of God is to heal people. Jesus touched a man who was considered untouchable and told him that He wanted him to be clean. And the leper was healed.

One day Jesus was in the synagogue on the Sabbath. There was a woman who had been bent over and infirm for eighteen years, and Jesus healed her so that she stood up straight and was no longer crippled.[202] Jesus used the miracle of healing the woman on the Sabbath to corroborate His testimony that as God He is Lord of the Sabbath.[203] The ruler of the synagogue was incensed that Jesus had broken their Sabbath tradition, but Jesus rebuked

---

[198] John 5:24-27.
[199] Exodus 7:9-12, 19-22, 8:1-7, 8:17-19.
[200] Revelation 13:13-18.
[201] Luke 5:12-13.
[202] Luke 13:11-13.
[203] Luke 6:5.

him for being a hypocrite because even he worked on the Sabbath to care for his animals.

On another Sabbath, Jesus healed the man who had been crippled for thirty-eight years lying at the pool of Bethesda. Jesus told the man, *"Rise, take up thy bed, and walk."*[204] Again, Jesus is performing a miracle for both of the reasons that were enumerated earlier. He had compassion on the man who had been crippled so long, and healed him. He used the healing to corroborate His testimony that as Lord of Creation, He is Lord of the Sabbath. When the Jews objected to the man's healing, Jesus told them that God, His Father, was working, therefore He was working. The Jews ignored the corroboration of the miracle showing that Jesus is Lord of the Sabbath, and instead took up stones to kill Him for blasphemy.

Once again, Jesus asserts His authority as Lord of the Sabbath and confirms that authority with a miracle of healing. On the Sabbath, a man was in the synagogue that had a withered hand.[205] Jesus had the man step forward and then asked the rulers and people of the synagogue if it was lawful to do good on the Sabbath. They refused to answer Him. The Gospel of Mark tells us that Jesus looked around at them with anger, being grieved because of the hardness of their hearts. He told the man with the withered hand to stretch his hand forth, and it was healed. Jesus' miracle healing of the man with the withered hand testified to the Jews that Jesus was Lord of the Sabbath and the God that heals them.

When Jesus was on his way to Jerusalem for the last time, on His way to suffer crucifixion on the cross, they were passing through Jericho, and a blind man named Bartimaeus, the son of Timaeus, sat by the roadside begging.[206] When the crowd was passing by he asked them what was happening and they told him

---

[204] John 5:1-9, 16-18.

[205] Mark 3:3-5.

[206] Mark 10:46-52; Luke 18:35-43.

that Jesus of Nazareth was there. Bartimaeus began calling out to Jesus to have mercy on him, *"Jesus, thou Son of David, have mercy on me."* The crowd told him to be quiet, but he cried out all the more. Jesus stopped and commanded them to call Bartimaeus to come to Him.

It's interesting that in the account from the Gospel of Mark, he tells us that when Bartimaeus gets up to come to Jesus, he casts away his garment. Blind men lived by begging and probably didn't have very much that they owned. He was so sure that Jesus was the Messiah who could heal him that he threw away what might have been his only possession.

Jesus asked him what he wanted and he replied that he wanted to have his sight. Jesus told him that his faith had made him whole. Bartimaeus demonstrated his faith by calling Jesus the Son of David, which was an appellation of the Messiah. Bartimaeus was telling everyone that Jesus is the Messiah. Jesus demonstrated that the faith of Bartimaeus was correct by healing his blindness. Mark tells us that after Bartimaeus was healed, he followed Jesus.

One day when Jesus was speaking to the crowd, a ruler of the local synagogue, Jairus, came and worshipped Jesus and begged him to come and revive his daughter who had died. While on the way to revive the man's daughter a woman in the crowd who had been sick for twelve years with a flow of blood came up behind Jesus and touched His garment. She said within herself that if only she could touch Jesus she would be made well. She reached out to Jesus and was healed immediately. Jesus was in the middle of a large crowd, and when the woman touched His garment he stopped and said, *"Who touched me?"* The woman came forward and falling on her knees confessed what she had done. Jesus told her that her faith had made her well. Just like blind Bartimaeus, the woman believed that Jesus was the Messiah sent by God into the world, and His healing of her confirmed it.[207] It should be noted that

---

[207] Matthew 9:18-22; Luke 8:43-48.

someone who had an issue of blood was automatically unclean, she couldn't touch anyone nor could they touch her. Everything she sat on or laid on was unclean.[208] It was an incredible burden for her and her family and friends. Just like the leper that Jesus cleansed, the healing of the woman not only restored her to health, but also materially changed her life.

There are many other accounts in the Gospels of Jesus healing people's blindness, deafness, leprosy, the casting out of demons, etc. All of these healings and deliverances of Jesus confirmed the truth of His words.

After Jesus healed the woman with the issue of blood, He came to Jairus' house. The people were wailing and mourning over the death of Jairus' daughter, a girl of only twelve years of age. Jesus told the people that the girl was only sleeping and they all ridiculed him, knowing that she was dead. Jesus commanded them to send all of the people out of the house and He took Peter, James, and John, and Jairus and the girl's mother with Him up to where the dead girl was laid. He held her by the hand and commanded her to come back from the dead.[209]

The raising of the daughter of Jairus from the dead was corroboration of his words to the Pharisees saying the dead would hear His voice and live:

> *Verily, verily, I say unto you, the hour is coming, and now is, when the dead shall hear the voice of the Son of God: and they that hear shall live. For as the Father hath life in himself; so hath he given to the Son to have life in himself; and hath given him authority to execute judgment also, because he is the Son of man.* (John 5:25-27 KJV)

---

[208] Leviticus 15:25-27.
[209] Matthew 9:18-19, 23-25; Luke 8:41-42, 49-56.

On another day, Jesus and the disciples were entering into the city of Nain, when they came upon the funeral of the only son of a widow.[210] Luke tells us that when Jesus saw the widow whose only son had died that He had mercy on her. He called the pall bearers to let down the bier holding the body, and spoke to the dead man saying, *"Young man, I say unto thee, arise."* Jesus spoke to the dead man and he came back to life again corroborating His testimony that He is the author of life and has life within Himself.

One of the most profound miracles of Jesus was the resurrection of Lazarus from the dead.[211] Lazarus was the brother of Martha and Mary and lived in the city of Bethany. The Gospel of John tells us that it was Mary who anointed Jesus' feet with oil and wiped them with her hair. Lazarus fell sick and Mary and Martha sent word to Jesus asking Him to come and heal their brother, whom Jesus loved. John tells us that when Jesus got word, instead of coming right away, He stayed two more days where He was.

When Jesus returned to Bethany, Lazarus had already been dead four days. [212] Both Mary and Martha reproved Jesus for not coming earlier and healing their brother. Speaking to Martha:

> *Jesus said unto her, I am the resurrection, and the life:*
> *he that believeth in me, though he were dead, yet shall*
> *he live: and whosoever liveth and believeth in me shall*
> *never die. Believest thou this?* (John 11:25-26 KJV)

Martha acknowledged that she believed in the resurrection and knew that her brother Lazarus would live again on the last day. When Jesus told her that He is the resurrection and the life, she confessed that Jesus is the Christ, the Son of God.[213]

Jesus told them to take the stone away from the tomb and

---

[210] Luke 7:11-16 KJV.
[211] John 11.
[212] John 11:39.
[213] John 11:27.

then spoke to Lazarus, *"Lazarus come forth,"* and he came back from the dead.[214]

The miracle of Jesus calling Lazarus back from the dead was so powerful of a witness that even the priests and Pharisees in opposition to Christ acknowledged that he had done it. But even though the miracle confirmed the truth of Christ's testimony, they refused to believe in Him because they were afraid of losing their position as the leaders of Israel.[215] Instead of changing their hearts before the miracle corroboration of the truth of Christ, they plotted to kill Lazarus so that people wouldn't believe that Jesus was the Messiah, the King of Israel.[216]

One thing must be noted about the people that Jesus resurrected from the dead (the daughter of Jairus, the son of the widow of Nain, and Lazarus). At sometime in their future, they would die again just like every other person who has ever lived. But Jesus' promise that the hour was coming when the dead would hear His voice and be resurrected to life was not just a promise that He could bring someone back from the dead.[217] It was a promise that one day in the future when Christ returns, all of those who have given their lives to Christ, both those who've already died and those who are still living, will be resurrected to eternal life in an everlasting body.[218]

It has already been stated that Jesus claimed to be God when he forgave people. When He healed the cripple who had been brought to him by his four friends, He stated specifically that the miracle of the healing was to corroborate the truth that He has the power to forgive people of their sins.[219] And again, Jesus was using the miracle for two different reasons. He displayed his compassion

---

[214] John 11:43-44 KJV.
[215] John 11:47-48.
[216] John 12:10-11
[217] John 5:25-27.
[218] John 5:28-29.
[219] Luke 5:24.

in healing the man and He corroborated His words to the scribes and Pharisees.

Jesus continually claimed that His miracles were proof of the truth of His testimony.[220] After John the Baptist had been thrown into prison he was experiencing doubt about what was happening. He sent two of his disciples to Christ to ask Him to confirm that Jesus was really the Messiah. The disciples came while Jesus was healing people. Jesus told the disciples to report what they had seen when they returned to John the Baptist:

> *The blind receive their sight, and the lame walk,*
> *the lepers are cleansed, and the deaf hear, the dead*
> *are raised up, and the poor have the gospel preached*
> *to them. And blessed is he, whosoever shall not be*
> *offended in me.* (Matthew 11:5-6 KJV)

Jesus was pointing out that he was fulfilling a prophecy of Isaiah that God would come to His people and when He did people would be healed.[221] Jesus used the corroboration of His miracles to encourage John the Baptist in the truth that Jesus is the Messiah just as God had shown him.

Jesus said that He did what no other man has ever done. The truth of His miracles was so compelling of a testimony that anyone who disbelieved the clear evidence of them was exhibiting proof of their sin; they hate Christ and they hate God.[222] The miracles of Jesus corroborate His testimony that He is God, the Son of God, and the Messiah sent by God into the world. They prove that Jesus spoke the truth and whoever ignores Him is in deadly peril.[223]

---

[220] John 5:36, 10:37-38, 14:10-11.

[221] Isaiah 35:4-6.

[222] John 15:24.

[223] John 12:48.

5.2.2 The Resurrection of Christ

The overriding or overarching miracle that corroborates the testimony of Christ is His own resurrection from the dead. It is the one miracle that stands above every other miracle and is the one miracle that Jesus promised would be given to all mankind as a sign of the truth of Christ.

Many people have written on the reasons to believe that the descriptions of the resurrection of Christ in the New Testament were truthful reporting by eyewitnesses. Most of these arguments for the resurrection are well known, and I'm just going to summarize them here. See the sources listed in the Appendix for some representative books that go into more detail for these arguments.

The evidence for the resurrection of Christ comes basically from four areas, the empty tomb, the eyewitness testimony of the disciples, the martyrdom of the apostles who refused to deny the resurrection even when faced with death, and the birth and growth of the Christian church in the years after His resurrection in the first century AD.

Some people say that Jesus didn't really die on the cross, that He was only wounded by the crucifixion, but revived while lying in the tomb. They ignore the fact that the Romans declared Christ dead and ensured that it was so when they stabbed Him in his side while hanging on the cross. John tells us that he witnessed blood and water flow out of the stab wound. The soldiers broke the legs of the other two criminals crucified on either side of Christ to hasten their death. Hanging on the cross asphyxiated a person and the only way to exhale was to lift up on his legs. Breaking their legs made it so they couldn't breathe and they died within a few minutes. Jesus was already dead, so they stabbed Him in the side through the lung and heart as assurance. The blood and the water (the pericardial and pleural effusion, a clear liquid that appears like water) came out from the heart and lung.[224] Roman law held the Roman guards responsible to receive the same punishment a prisoner was due if they let him escape. The Roman executioners would not have allowed a condemned Jesus to come down off of the cross alive. Jesus was dead when they took him down off of the cross, and laid him in the tomb. Pilate confirmed his death with the Roman Centurion before releasing His body to burial.[225]

The first area of evidence supporting the resurrection is the empty tomb. Some people claim that the disciples were confused where the body of Jesus was laid, and when they proclaimed His resurrection because of the empty tomb, they were really in the wrong place. They say that Jesus was dead and interred in a different tomb. That argument flies in the face of the statements of the disciples that they had seen the resurrected Jesus. They had touched him and eaten with him. Also, the Gospel of Luke explicitly states that the disciples saw the tomb where they laid Jesus' body.[226]

The Bible tells us that the rulers of the Jews knew about Jesus' claim that He would be resurrected and they asked Pilate to set a guard on the tomb so that the disciples of Christ couldn't steal His body away and claim that He had been resurrected.[227] So they sealed the stone in front of the tomb and set a group of soldiers to guard the tomb until the three days had passed. On the day of the resurrection of Jesus the stone was rolled away from the tomb and when the disciples entered the tomb they found it empty of the body of Christ, it only contained His burial wrappings.[228] *The Bible* tells us that an angel came down from heaven and rolled away the stone. When the angel appeared, the soldiers guarding the tomb were struck down in fright and later went and told the

---

[224] John 19:34.
[225] Mark 15:44-45.
[226] Luke 23:55.
[227] Matthew 27:62-66.
[228] John 20:3-10.

rulers of Israel what had happened. They bribed the guards to say that the disciples had stolen the body of Jesus while they were asleep.[229] The reason the guards had to be bribed is because they faced the death penalty for sleeping while on watch if what they said turned out to be true.

It's interesting that *The Bible* reports that when John looked into the tomb and saw the linen burial wrappings lying there that he believed.[230] Why would just looking at the empty linen wrappings[231] cause John to believe? Maybe looking at the linen wrappings caused John to remember Jesus' words that He would be resurrected? Maybe there was something about the linen wrappings that revealed the miracle of Christ's resurrection? *The Bible* doesn't say, but when John looked into the tomb, he believed.

The tomb was empty and the rulers of Jerusalem wanted desperately to silence the testimony of the disciples as to the resurrection of Jesus. All the rulers had to do was produce the body of Jesus. Yet the rulers were unable to produce His body or refute the accounts of His resurrection. If Jesus were really dead the rulers would have produced His body as proof. They didn't produce His body because they couldn't. They had total control of the burial site. They had their own guards surrounding it.

The disciples were locked in an upper room for fear of the Jews.[232] The disciples were afraid that the same thing that happened to Jesus was going to happen to them. They didn't overpower the guards and steal Jesus' body. Jesus was resurrected from the dead. He is alive today.

A few years ago there was a documentary produced purporting to have found the tomb of Jesus with His body inside[233]. The only

---

[229] Matthew 28:2-4, 11-15.
[230] John 20:5,8.
[231] Luke 24:12.
[232] John 20:19.
[233] *https://en.wikipedia.org/wiki/The_Lost_Tomb_of_Jesus*. See also: *http://www.huffingtonpost.com/richard-w-kropf/the-tomb-of-jesus-and-the_b_5187390.html*

tomb of Jesus is the empty tomb in the garden. There will never be a tomb found with the body of Jesus because He is alive today.

The second area of evidence for the resurrection of Jesus is the eyewitness testimony of those who saw Christ alive after His death. Before the resurrection of Christ, the disciples were locked in the upper room hiding from the Jewish leaders for fear. After they saw Jesus alive, they were boldly going around and witnessing to everyone that He had been resurrected. On the day of Pentecost over three thousand people became followers of Christ when they heard Peter testify that Jesus was the Christ and had been resurrected in accordance with prophecy, and that the disciples were eyewitnesses to the resurrection of Christ.[234] Later, when going to the temple for afternoon prayers, God used Peter and John to heal a man who had been lame from birth. Peter used the occasion of the man's healing to preach the resurrection of Christ, telling the people that Jesus is the Messiah promised to them and that God had raised Him from the dead.[235]

Peter told Cornelius and all of the gentile believers at his house that God raised Jesus from the dead, and they were witnesses to His resurrection. He also told them that God hadn't shown Jesus alive to everyone, but to those witnesses that God had chosen beforehand. Peter's testimony that they were eyewitnesses to the resurrection wasn't just that they had seen Jesus alive after his crucifixion, but that they had been with the resurrected Christ for a lengthy period of time and they had eaten and drunk with Jesus.[236]

Peter confirmed the resurrection when he wrote his first epistle. He said that God had given them a living hope by the resurrection of Jesus Christ from the dead.[237] Peter and all of the

---

[234] Acts 2:30-32.
[235] Acts 3:12-16,26.
[236] Acts 10:38-41.
[237] 1 Peter 1:3.

disciples of Christ were born again to a living hope in God because of the resurrection.

Paul testified to the Greeks in Athens that God had resurrected Christ from the dead to let all people know that there was a day of judgment coming and Jesus Christ would be the judge.[238] Paul testified before King Agrippa that Jesus appeared to him on the road to Damascus and meeting Jesus face-to-face changed his life. When Paul told King Agrippa about the resurrection of Jesus from the dead he testified that these things had not been done in secret, and King Agrippa was well aware of them.[239] Paul was confirming something that everyone had heard about by stating that he was also a witness to the resurrection.

Some people discount Paul's eyewitness account of the resurrection of Jesus because Jesus had already ascended to heaven. They say that when Jesus appeared to Paul in a vision it was a spiritual appearance and not a physical one. However, Paul confirmed the physical resurrection of Christ when he wrote to the Corinthians and told them that there were over five hundred people still alive who had witnessed the resurrection of Christ in the flesh, implying that they could confirm his testimony by speaking to any of those still living who had witnessed the resurrection.[240] Paul testifies in many of his epistles to the resurrection of Jesus Christ from the dead.[241]

The apostles Matthew and John, who were eyewitnesses of the resurrection of Christ, testify to the resurrection in the Gospels.[242] The Gospels of Luke and Mark record the testimony of eyewitnesses.

Nothing is known of Luke prior to his appearing as a travel companion of Paul in the book of Acts. It is assumed that Luke is

---

[238] Acts 17:30-31.

[239] Acts 26:13-18,22-26.

[240] 1 Corinthians 15:3-8.

[241] Galatians 1:1; Ephesians 1:17-21; Colossians 1:18; 1 Thessalonians 1:10.

[242] Matthew 28:1-8,16-20; John 20:26-31, 21:14.

with Paul starting in Acts 21 because of his use of the pronoun, "*we.*" But there is not a direct statement from Luke that he was an eyewitness to the resurrection of Jesus. It can be inferred that he was an eyewitness because of the opening prologue of his Gospel. He testifies that he had perfect knowledge of what he recounts from the very beginning.[243]

Mark, also called John Mark, was a companion of Paul,[244] and early Church tradition says that Mark was also a companion of Peter. Mark was on the scene from very early. The disciples were praying at the house of his mother, Mary, when Peter was arrested by Herod and was in prison under sentence of death.[245] Some people postulate that the identity of the young man who fled naked from the garden of Gethsemane was Mark, although there is no way to know for certain.[246] But the story is only recounted in Mark's Gospel. If it was Mark who fled naked the night Jesus was arrested, then his Gospel is more than just the recording of other eyewitnesses to the resurrection of Christ, it was also a recording of Mark's eyewitness to the resurrection.

Every one of the apostles except for John was martyred for their testimony that Jesus was resurrected from the dead, and John was tortured and exiled to the island of Patmos. They could have recanted and saved their lives but everyone of them suffered death. *Foxe's Book of Martyrs*[247] describes the deaths of many of the apostles and disciples. In times past there have been people who went to their death believing a lie. But no one, knowing the truth will sacrifice his life for a lie. All of the apostles were in a position to know the truth and they refused to recant their testimony

---

[243] Luke 1:1-4.

[244] Acts 12:25; 2 Timothy 4:11.

[245] Acts 12:1-12.

[246] Mark 14:51-52.

[247] *Actes and Monuments* by John Foxe, commonly referred to by the name, *Foxe's Book of Martyrs*. Published in 1563 by John Day.

confirming the resurrection of Jesus Christ from the dead, but rather maintained to the end that Jesus Christ is alive.

The final argument for the resurrection is the fact of the birth and growth of the Christian church. At the time of the crucifixion of Jesus, there were only 120 disciples still following Him.[248] Everyone else had deserted Him. They were amazed by His miracles, they accepted His healings, they were filled by His food,[249] but they were unwilling to follow Him because it meant being made outcasts by the Jewish leaders.[250] It meant denying themselves to follow Him.[251] It meant suffering and tribulation,[252] and they were unwilling.

Earlier during Christ' ministry a number of disciples deserted Him and no longer followed him because they didn't understand his teaching about being the bread of life.[253] Jesus asked the disciples if they also wanted to leave Him:

> Then said Jesus unto the twelve, – Will ye also go away? Then Simon Peter answered him, Lord, to whom shall we go? Thou hast the words of eternal life. And we believe and are sure that thou art that Christ, the Son of the living God. (John 6:67-69 KJV)

In only a few days the fact of the resurrection of Christ changed a small body of fearful disciples into a large number of bold followers of Christ willing to suffer beatings and imprisonments for his name. On the day of Pentecost, fifty days after the crucifixion of Christ, when the Holy Spirit fell on the disciples, Peter preached a sermon testifying to the truth of the resurrection and three

---

[248] Acts 1:15.
[249] John 6:26-27.
[250] John 9:20-22, 12:42.
[251] Luke 9:23.
[252] John 15:17-21.
[253] John 6:48-63.

thousand people were added to their number.[254] Upon their first arrest, Peter's boldness, boldness that came from witnessing the resurrection of Christ and the filling of the Holy Spirit, led him to tell the Jewish council:

> *Neither is there salvation in any other: for there is none other name under heaven given among men, whereby we must be saved.* (Acts 4:10-12 KJV)

Peter and John were uneducated fishermen who stood up to the ruling council of the Jews, and when they were arrested a second time refused their order to quit preaching in Jesus' name. They reported the resurrection of Christ to the council and received a beating rather than submit to their order.[255] The growth of the church was built on the lives of those who were imprisoned and martyred for refusing to recant the truth of the resurrection of Christ.[256]

The power of the truth of the resurrection and the anointing of the Holy Spirit on the disciples was so great that the people around them feared them and magnified them.[257] In only a few years Christianity spread throughout all of Israel, Turkey, Greece, and all of Asia,[258] during a time when the Jews were imprisoning and killing anyone who claimed the name of Christ. That growth was directly attributable to the fact of the resurrection of Christ.

Before Paul met Christ on the road to Damascus, he was leading the persecution of the followers of Christ.[259] He had received warrants from the Pharisees in Jerusalem to go to Damascus and

---

[254] Acts 2:41.
[255] Acts 5:29-32,40.
[256] Acs 7:55-60, 8:1-3, 12:1-2.
[257] Acts 5:12-13.
[258] Acts 19:10.
[259] Acts 8:3.

arrest anyone who was following Christ.[260] Jesus appeared to Paul and stopped his persecution of the church. Paul was blinded by the glory of Christ and was led by hand to Damascus. God sent a disciple named Ananias to lay hands on Paul and heal his blindness.[261]

That meeting with the living Christ changed Paul forever, and he immediately started proclaiming both the resurrection and the fact that Jesus is the Messiah.[262] The Jews persecuted Paul his entire life, beating him, stoning him, and hounding him out of their cities.[263] At one point a group of Jews entered into a curse, saying that would eat and drink nothing until they killed him.[264] Yet through all of it, the knowledge that Jesus had been resurrected and was alive caused Paul to stand against everyone who denied the truth of Christ's resurrection. Paul said that he counted everything that he had as no more than rubbish so that he could have Christ.[265]

If Christ had not been resurrected, the church would have died with him. Gamaliel, one of the members of the Jewish Sanhedrin warned the Jews to be careful how they treated the disciples of Christ. If Jesus were just a man, his followers would fall away, just as happened to every other movement after their leader died.[266] But, the resurrection proved that it was Christ working to build his church,[267] and the church grew exponentially.

As a final comment about the resurrection of Christ, it's interesting to note that *The Bible* says that all three persons of the Trinity cooperated in the resurrection of Christ. *The Bible*

---

[260] Acts 9:1-9.
[261] Acts 9:10-19.
[262] Acts 9:20-22.
[263] 2 Corinthians 11:24-28.
[264] Acts 23:12-13.
[265] Philippians 3:8.
[266] Acts 5:34-39.
[267] Matthew 16:18.

tells us that God the Father resurrected Jesus;[268] the Holy Spirit resurrected Jesus;[269] and Jesus would resurrect Himself.[270] The work of the resurrection was the work of the Trinity in perfect cooperation, carrying out the will of God in the salvation of mankind.

The miracle of the resurrection of Jesus is the corroboration that He is the Son of God, the Christ, the Messiah, and that everything that He said was true.

5.3 The Corroboration of God the Father

The third witness that corroborates the testimony of Jesus is God the Father. Jesus said:

> *And the Father Himself, who sent Me, has testified of Me. You have neither heard His voice at any time, nor seen His form. But you do not have His word abiding in you, because whom He sent, Him you do not believe.* (John 5:37-38 NKJV)

Although all of Scripture could be called the corroboration of God the Father that Jesus is the Christ, the term is going to be used to mean those times when God gave explicit witness to people in the New Testament in confirmation of Jesus as His Son, the Messiah. So, to whom did God reveal what He was doing? What did He have to say in corroboration of the testimony of Christ?

---

[268] Hebrews 13:20.
[269] Romans 8:11.
[270] John 2:19.

5.3.1 God Testified to Mary

God testified to Mary through the angel Gabriel.[271] Not only had He told her that as a virgin she was going to conceive a child, but He specifically told her that the child conceived, Jesus, would be the Son of God, and that He would be the king who sat on the throne of David in fulfillment of God's promise to David.[272] Mary was confused at his testimony because although she was betrothed to Joseph, they weren't yet married. The marriage had not been consummated. Gabriel told her that she would conceive in her womb by the power of the Holy Spirit of God.

What was the response of Mary to the testimony of God?

> *And Mary said, behold the handmaid of the Lord; be*
> *it unto me according to thy word...* (Luke 1:38a KJV)

Mary declared that she was the handmaid, or servant, of the Lord, and accepted whatever the will of God was for her. Her humbling herself under the will of God no matter what the consequences were for her own life was at the root of why she would be blessed by all generations.[273]

God then corroborated the truth of His testimony to Mary by her being pregnant and giving birth to Jesus even though she had never known a man. It was done unto Mary according to God's word. Mary knew that God had spoken the truth to her and lived in wonder at what other things God was going to reveal to her, and pondered all of those things in her heart.[274]

---

[271] Luke 1:26-38.
[272] 2 Samuel 7:8-16.
[273] Luke 1:46-50.
[274] Luke 2:19.

5.3.2 God Testified to Joseph

Mary and Joseph were betrothed, and God had chosen both of them and given them the responsibility to raise Jesus up and watch over Him while He was young. God didn't only testify to Mary who Jesus was. God testified to Joseph also, to ensure that there would never be any bitterness between them over Mary having a baby that Joseph hadn't fathered. The Angel of the Lord appeared to Joseph in a dream and told him that Mary was pregnant by the Holy Spirit. The Angel of the Lord told Joseph the name of the baby, Jesus. Furthermore, He told Joseph the reason for the name, *"For he shall save his people from their sins."* Then Joseph took Mary as his wife, but abstained from sexual relations with her until after the birth of Jesus.[275]

5.3.3 God Testified to Elizabeth

God testified to Elizabeth, Mary's cousin and the mother of John the Baptist. When God sent the angel Gabriel to Zacharias to announce the birth of John the Baptist, he promised that John would be filled with the Holy Spirit from the womb.[276] When Mary went to visit Elizabeth after the conception of Jesus, Elizabeth and John in her womb were filled with the Holy Spirit. The Holy Spirit revealed to Elizabeth that Mary was the mother of the Lord Christ, and Elizabeth called Mary, *"The mother of my Lord,"* and promised Mary that the Lord would perform the things that had been told her.[277] Elizabeth's testimony was another corroborating witness to Mary as to the truth of the testimony that God had given to her.

---

[275] Matthew 1:19-25.
[276] Luke 1:15.
[277] Luke 1:40-45.

5.3.4 God Testified to the Shepherds

An angel of the Lord testified to the shepherds in the fields to the birth of the Christ. The angel told the shepherds that the Christ was born that day in the city of Bethlehem, and that they would find Him lying in a manger. The shepherds then went to Bethlehem to see if what the angel told them was the truth, and they found Jesus and Mary in the manger just as the angel had said. They told Mary and everyone else who was there that the angel had revealed to them that the baby Jesus was the Messiah and that they could find Him in Bethlehem, and they had been witnesses to the glory of God and of the angels singing praises.[278]

5.3.5 God Testified to Simeon

God testified to His servant Simeon in the temple in Jerusalem. The Holy Spirit promised Simeon that he wouldn't die until he saw the Messiah, the Christ. So one morning, prompted by the Holy Spirit he went to the temple. The law stated that when a male child was born, his mother would be unclean for seven days. On the eighth day the boy would be circumcised. The mother of the boy would continue in her purification for thirty-three days. At the end of that period, they were to take a sacrifice to the temple and present the boy to the Lord.[279] Mary and Joseph had circumcised the baby Jesus on the eighth day and then brought Jesus to the temple to dedicate Him to the Lord at the end of Mary's days of purification. The Holy Spirit witnessed to Simeon that Jesus was the Christ and Simeon acknowledged that when he said that he had seen the salvation of God in Jesus, in confirmation of the word of God to him. Again, the statements of Simeon, confirming the

---

[278] Luke 2:8-18.
[279] Exodus 13:2; Leviticus 12.

testimony of God were corroboration to Mary of the truth of the testimony of God to her.[280]

5.3.6 God Testified to the Wise Men

God caused a star to shine that the wise men of the east interpreted as a sign of the birth of the Messiah, and they traveled to Israel to find the Messiah.[281] Some people postulate that the wise men from the east were from a school of prophets in Persia that had been founded by Daniel five hundred years earlier and this is why they were searching the scriptures for the fulfillment of the prophecies of Daniel. The documentary video, *The Star of Bethlehem*[282] states that it was also believed that in very early times before men started worshipping the stars through astrology, that God wrote the salvation story in the stars and that the wise men were interpreting that. It is unknown whether this is true, but it must be asked, why did the wise men interpret the star as a sign of the birth of the Messiah? In the corroboration of the testimony of John the Baptist, everyone was looking for the coming of the Messiah according to Daniel's seventy weeks of years prophecy.[283] The wise men must have been believers in the truth of the Scriptures and had been searching for the fulfillment of them.

Whatever the reason, the wise men faithfully followed that star to Jerusalem and went into King Herod's court on the basis of their interpretation, and asked Herod where had the King of the Jews been born. King Herod asked the scribes and they told him that it was prophesied that the King of the Jews would be born in Bethlehem.[284]

---

[280] Luke 2:25-35.

[281] Matthew 2:1-18.

[282] "The Star of Bethlehem by Frederick A. "Rick" Larson, directed by Stephen Vidano. Copyright ã 2007.

[283] Daniel 9:24-26.

[284] Micah 5:2.

The wise men found Jesus in Bethlehem and presented Him with gifts fit for the Son of God, the King of Israel, who was going to give His life as a sacrifice. Frankincense was a consecrated incense used in the temple worship of God.[285] The frankincense was an acknowledgment that Jesus is the Son of God. Myrrh was a spice used to make the anointing oil that the Levitical priests used in the worship and consecration of the temple.[286] It was to be reserved for the use of God only. Any man who compounded any anointing oil like it was under sentence of death. The myrrh was an acknowledgment of the purpose of God in Christ, His atoning death. Nicodemus and Joseph of Arimathea used it when they wrapped the body of Jesus for burial in the tomb.[287] The gold was a gift acknowledging that the Messiah was the King of Israel.

God warned the wise men in a dream not to return to Jerusalem or tell King Herod that they had found the Messiah, and they returned home by a different way. God warned Joseph to flee with Mary and Jesus to Egypt, and in anger King Herod killed all of the male children two years old and younger to try to protect his throne.[288]

Many people have rejected the testimony of God in respect to the star leading the wise men to Jesus, saying stars don't move, the motion of a comet doesn't explain the testimony, etc. Referring again to the documentary movie, *The Star of Bethlehem*, mentioned earlier, the movie seeks to show that the testimony of God concerning the star is true. The producers of the movie used modern astronomical software to rollback the heavens to the way they were at the time of the birth of Christ and then examine the sky to try to understand this testimony. They claim that the Star of Bethlehem was what has sometimes been called a wandering star,

---

[285] Exodus 30:34-38.
[286] Exodus 30:22-33.
[287] John 19:38-40.
[288] Matthew 2:16-18; Jeremiah 31:15.

which in reality was the planet Jupiter. It stopped over Bethlehem during its retrograde motion.

5.3.7 God Testified to John the Baptist

God testified of His Son to John the Baptist when Jesus was baptized. John heard the voice of God saying, *"This is my beloved Son, in whom I am well pleased."*[289] John also stated that God told him that on whomever he saw the Holy Spirit descend and remain on him was the Christ, the one who baptizes with the Holy Spirit.[290] John witnessed the Holy Spirit alighting on Christ when he baptized him.

5.3.8 God Testified to Peter, James, and John

God testified to Peter, James, and John on the Mount of Transfiguration. Jesus had prophesied that some of His disciples would not taste death until they saw the kingdom of heaven. A week later, Jesus led Peter, James, and John up on a mountain to pray. While He was praying He was transformed, His face was altered, His clothes became whiter than was humanly possible, and the glory of God shone around them. Moses and Elijah came and talked with Him concerning His upcoming death on the cross. Peter was bewildered and afraid and spoke without thinking, telling Jesus that the disciples would make three tabernacles, one for Jesus, one for Moses, and one for Elijah. In essence, Peter was abasing Jesus, putting Him on the same level as Moses and Elijah. A cloud of the glory of the Lord overshadowed them, and God Himself spoke to them, *"This is my beloved Son: hear him."* God

---

[289] Mark 1:17 NKJV.
[290] John 1:31-34.

corrected Peter's error and confirmed that Jesus is the Son of God to the disciples, which also meant that Jesus is the Christ.[291]

5.3.9 God Testified to the Disciples

One day during the week before Jesus was crucified, when Jesus was troubled and looking ahead to what He was going to suffer, He prayed that God would glorify His name through His sacrifice. God replied to Jesus and all of the disciples heard him. He told Jesus, *"I have both glorified it, and will glorify it again."* Jesus told the disciples that God spoke for their sakes, so that they would know that Jesus is the Christ and everything that was going to happen was according to the will of God and for the glory of God.[292]

5.3.10 God Testified to the Women at the Tomb

After the resurrection of Jesus, God sent angels to the tomb to testify to the women who were looking to complete His anointing for burial.[293] In the Jewish culture of the day, women weren't considered reliable witnesses.[294] Yet God chose to corroborate His testimony to them showing that He considered them reliable witnesses.

5.3.11 God Testified to All Mankind

Finally, the resurrection of Christ is God's testimony that Jesus is the Messiah, the King of Israel and of all of creation. Paul told us that the resurrection of Christ is the witness of God that Jesus

---

[291] Luke 9:27-35 KJV.

[292] John 12:27-33 KJV.

[293] Luke 24:4-7.

[294] Luke 24:9-11.

Christ is the Son of God and will sit on the seat of judgment on the last day.[295]

> *Truly, these times of ignorance God overlooked,*
> *but now commands all men everywhere to repent,*
> *because He has appointed a day on which He will*
> *judge the world in righteousness by the Man whom*
> *He has ordained. He has given assurance of this to*
> *all by raising Him from the dead."* (Acts 17:30-31
> NKJV)

God Himself authenticated the testimony of Jesus.

5.4 The Corroboration of Scripture

Jesus rebuked the Pharisees for claiming that they believed the Scriptures, but didn't believe in Jesus whom the Scriptures witnessed to:

> *You search the Scriptures, for in them you think you*
> *have eternal life; and these are they which testify of*
> *Me.* (John 5:39 NKJV)

When Jesus speaks of the witness of Scripture, He was referring to the Scriptures that the Jews had access to at the time He was speaking to them, what Christians refer to as the Old Testament. Jesus specifically told the Pharisees that Moses had written about Him, and the writings of Moses[296] would be their accusers when they stood before God:

---

[295] Romans 1:1-4.
[296] Genesis, Exodus, Leviticus, Numbers, and Deuteronomy.

> *Do not think that I will accuse you to the Father:*
> *there is one that accuseth you, even Moses, in whom*
> *ye trust. For had ye believed Moses, ye would have*
> *believed me: for he wrote of me. But if ye believe not*
> *his writings, how shall ye believe my words?* (John
> 5:45-47 KJV)

Jesus confirmed that the Old Testament was a witness to himself when speaking with the disciples on the road to Emmaus.[297]

God gave prophecies of who the Messiah would be and why he would come. The prophecies of the Messiah are the promises of God that He was going to provide a cleansing for sin, a redemption for people, so that they could be saved from the wrath of God against sin. The Messiah would be the salvation of all peoples, not just the Jews only, but for the gentile nations as well.

God foretold specific details about the coming of the Messiah so that the people could authenticate that He really was the Messiah, the anointed one of God. The prophecies were given so that people could know the truth.

The work of God in sending the Messiah to the earth would not be just something that He did. God was in unity with the Son of God and the Holy Spirit in the mission of the Messiah. This is corroborated in the testimony of the Messiah himself given through the inspiration of the Holy Spirit to David:

> *Then said I, Lo, I come: in the volume of the book it*
> *is written of me, I delight to do thy will, O my God:*
> *yea, thy law is within my heart. I have preached*
> *righteousness in the great congregation: lo, I have*
> *not refrained my lips, O Lord, thou knowest. I have*
> *not hid thy righteousness within my heart; I have*
> *declared thy faithfulness and thy salvation: I have not*

---

[297] Luke 24:25-27.

concealed thy lovingkindness and thy truth from the great congregation. (Psalms 40:7-10 KJV)

It was in the heart of the Messiah to carry out the will of God, because God's law was written there.[298] His purpose was to witness to the righteousness and truth of God; to show people the salvation of God. The heart of the Messiah was to show people the love and mercy of God towards them.

Mankind had sold himself into sin and slavery when he had believed Satan and rebelled against God.[299] The purpose of God in sending the Messiah was so that mankind could know who God is and know the truth of what God had spoken, to refute the lies of Satan.[300] The purpose of God in sending the Messiah was to destroy Satan and his works.[301] The Messiah was going to redeem mankind from sin and slavery with the price of his own blood.[302] The Messiah was going to restore to man the image of God that he lost when he rebelled.[303]

The Messiah would be a prophet, speaking the words of God. Whoever would not listen to Him would be destroyed.[304] The Messiah would be a priest forever, the only intercessor between God and man.[305] The Messiah would be made the ruler of all creation. God prophesied that the Messiah would sit in judgment of all nations.[306] The establishment of His kingdom would destroy all other kingdoms and He would reign supreme forever.[307]

There is one characteristic of God that is unique to Him. God

---

[298] Psalms 40:7-8.
[299] Genesis 3:1-19.
[300] John 18:36-37.
[301] Hebrews 2:14.
[302] 1 Peter 1:18-19.
[303] 2 Corinthians 3:18.
[304] Deuteronomy 18:18-19.
[305] Psalms 110:4.
[306] Psalms 2:6-9.
[307] Daniel 2:44, 7:14.

is the only one who can foretell the future. No created being, man, angel, or demon can foresee the future. God said that the test of a prophet, whether he is from God or not, is that 100% of what he prophesies comes to pass.[308] Demons and men prognosticate about the future with mixed results. They make guesses based upon the character of people, the culture, and current events, but only God knows the future. God says in Isaiah that this is the proof that only He is God.[309]

When God reveals future events by prophecy in the Old Testament, and only Jesus fulfills those events, it is the corroboration of scripture that Jesus is the Christ, sent from God.

5.4.1 The Characteristics of the Messiah

The Old Testament is a picture of the Messiah that God painted. At first there are just some penciled in marks defining the boundaries of the painting. But then God begins to paint with oil and brush on the canvas of history through the prophets. An image of the Messiah from the heart of God emerges, a God who loves His creation, and wants to redeem it from the curse of sin.

At the time of the rebellion of Adam and Eve, God pronounced a curse on Satan, the serpent. Satan's desire was to be made higher than God, to exalt himself over all of creation.[310] God told Satan that he is going to be made lower than every other created being because of his instigation of the rebellion of mankind.[311]

The curse on Satan is the first prophecy God gives us of the Messiah. God tells us that someone was coming who was going to crush Satan's head. And in majestic irony, God says that someone will be the seed of the woman. Satan had deceived the woman

---

[308] Deuteronomy 18:21-22.
[309] Isaiah 46:9-10.
[310] Isaiah 14:13-15.
[311] Genesis 3:14.

and used her to foster the rebellion of Adam, so God was going to use a woman in the downfall of Satan:

> *And I will put enmity between thee and the woman, and between thy seed and her seed; it shall bruise thy head, and thou shalt bruise his heel.* (Genesis 3:15 KJV)

Alexander Hislop, in his seminal work on idolatry, *The Two Babylons*,[312] states that the birth of idolatry was in the kingdom of Nimrod. Nimrod claimed that he was the fulfillment of the prophecy to bruise the serpent's head, he was the one prophesied to save mankind. In one sense, idolatry has always been someone stealing the glory of God and the work that God is doing, and claiming it for themselves. Throughout history various idolatrous religions have used symbols of a snake underfoot, claiming that they are the ones that have been victorious over the serpent. But no ordinary man could ever overcome Satan in his own power. It would take someone more powerful than Satan to defeat and destroy him. The Messiah would be the anointed one of God sent to conquer Satan. Satan wouldn't be defeated using the wisdom or strength of men. Satan is wiser and stronger than men. The Messiah, the Son of God would defeat Satan using God's wisdom and God's power in obedience to God's will.

The next reference to the Messiah is when God made a promise to Abraham to give him an everlasting heritage. God promised Abraham that his seed would be more than the stars in the sky and the sand of the seashore, and that through his seed all of the nations of the earth would be blessed.

---

[312] "The Two Babylons," by Reverend Alexander Hislop. 1858. Available on Amazon Kindle.

> *And the angel of the Lord called unto Abraham out*
> *of heaven the second time, and said, by myself have I*
> *sworn, saith the Lord, for because thou hast done this*
> *thing, and hast not withheld thy son, thine only son:*
> *that in blessing I will bless thee, and in multiplying I*
> *will multiply thy seed as the stars of the heaven, and*
> *as the sand which is upon the sea shore; and thy seed*
> *shall possess the gate of his enemies; and in thy seed*
> *shall all the nations of the earth be blessed; because*
> *thou hast obeyed my voice.* (Genesis 22:17-18 KJV)

How would the seed of Abraham bless all nations? God would use Israel in two ways. First, Israel was going to be a witness to God. God was going to have Israel record His dealings with them; they were going to record who He is and what He had spoken. Israel would record the picture of the Messiah that God painted. Israel would record God's word, *The Bible*, and give it to the world, so that God could reveal Himself to people throughout history. God meant for the truth of His word to bless all generations.[313]

Second, the Messiah would come from the seed of Abraham through the lineage of Israel and He would be a blessing to all mankind, because he would save mankind from their sins and from the wrath of God to come. A thousand years after Abraham, God showed the prophet Isaiah how the Messiah would be a blessing to all nations. God said that His soul would delight in His servant, His chosen one, the Messiah. The Messiah would execute justice in righteousness. The anointing of God in the form of the Holy Spirit would rest on the Messiah.[314] John the Baptist witnessed to this when speaking of Jesus.[315] The Messiah would speak the words of God and the Holy Spirit would be poured out

---

[313] Psalms 100:5.

[314] Isaiah 42:1-4.

[315] John 3:34.

on him without measure. He would free those held in prison and open the eyes of those who were blind. The Messiah would bring the light of God to all mankind. He would be given as a covenant to the gentiles, a promise from God of forgiveness and salvation:

> *I the Lord have called thee in righteousness, and will hold thine hand, and will keep thee, and give thee for a covenant of the people, for a light of the Gentiles; to open the blind eyes, to bring out the prisoners from the prison, and them that sit in darkness out of the prison house.* (Isaiah 42:6-7 KJV)

God gave this prophecy of the Messiah 700 years before the birth of Jesus Christ, and specifically stated in the prophecy that He was giving it so that everyone would know that He alone is God.[316] When people witnessed the fulfillment of the prophecy, it would prove that the Lord, "YHWH," was the only God.

Jesus stated to the apostles on the night before His crucifixion that His blood shed on the cross was the blood of the new covenant between God and man,[317] the blood sealing the covenant, which God promised to all people in the person of the Messiah.

Looking back at the history described in the Old Testament, it is clear that God established three offices for the people he had chosen to serve Him, the office of the prophet, the office of the priest, and the office of the king. Sometimes there is a crossover between the offices of prophet and priest, or between king and prophet. But never is there anyone who occupies the office of all three except for the Messiah.

Moses was a prophet called by God but he also acted as a priest, glorifying God before the people, and representing the people before God. He acted in the office of priest when sanctifying the

---

[316] Isaiah 42:5,8-9.
[317] Matthew 26:28

tabernacle and Aaron and his sons to be priests. Samuel was called by God to be a prophet, but God also used him in the office of priest to make sacrifices before God. King Saul tried to usurp the office of priest from Samuel when he offered the sacrifices instead of waiting for Samuel.[318] Saul wasn't the only king of Israel who tried to usurp the office of priest; King Uzziah of Judah did the same thing and was struck with leprosy for his presumption.[319] David was anointed as the king of Israel, but as a prophet of God was filled with the Holy Spirit, and wrote many prophetic words in the book of Psalms.[320] Solomon was chosen to stand in the office of king of Israel by God and was given the wisdom of a prophet by God that he recorded in the books of Proverbs, Ecclesiastes, and the Song of Solomon. Jeremiah was born a priest, but God took him at an early age and put him in the office of prophet.[321] Every legitimate prophet, priest, and king was anointed by God to fulfill the role each was called to.

5.4.1.1 The King of Creation

The Old Testament states that the Messiah would be the King of Israel and all of creation. The first prophecy of this is when Joseph is getting ready to die and prophesied over his sons. He singled out the tribe of his son, Judah, and says that they would rule and from them the Messiah would come:

> The sceptre shall not depart from Judah, nor a lawgiver from between his feet, until Shiloh come; and unto him shall the gathering of the people be. (Genesis 49:10 KJV)

---

[318] 1 Samuel 13.
[319] 2 Chronicles 26:16-21.
[320] 1 Samuel 16:13; Mark 12:36.
[321] Jeremiah 1:5.

Strong's Concordance says that the name *"Shiloh"*[322] in the above passage refers to the Messiah. The Messiah would be the lawgiver with the ruler's sceptre and come from the tribe of Judah.

God prophesied to Hannah, the mother of the prophet Samuel, that He would exalt His king, the Messiah:

> *He will keep the feet of his saints, and the wicked shall be silent in darkness; for by strength shall no man prevail. The adversaries of the Lord shall be broken to pieces; out of heaven shall he thunder upon them: the Lord shall judge the ends of the earth; and he shall give strength unto his king, and exalt the horn of his anointed. (1 Samuel 2:9-10)*

Again, notice that the Hebrew word translated *"anointed"* in this verse is *"masiyah"*, i.e., the Messiah.[323]

David was of the tribe of Judah.[324] When it was in David's heart to build a temple for God, a permanent dwelling place for Him in Jerusalem, God sent Nathan to David to tell him that his son Solomon would build a temple to God, not David. But then God told David that instead of David building a house for Him, God was going to build an everlasting kingdom for the seed of David and establish his throne forever.

> *And when thy days be fulfilled, and thou shalt sleep with thy fathers, I will set up thy seed after thee, which shall proceed out of thy bowels, and I will establish his kingdom. He shall build an house for my name, and I will stablish the throne of his kingdom for ever ... And thine house and thy kingdom shall be established*

---

[322] Strong's number h7886, *siylo*, an epithet of the Messiah.

[323] Strong's number h4899, *masiyah*.

[324] Ruth 4:18-22; 1 Chronicles 2:3-15.

> *for ever before thee: thy throne shall be established for*
> *ever.* (2 Samuel 7:12-13,16 KJV)

> *The Lord hath sworn in truth unto David; he will not*
> *turn from it; of the fruit of thy body will I set upon thy*
> *throne.* (Psalm 132:11 KJV)

Some commentators take these verses from 2 Samuel to apply to Solomon only, for he built the first temple. However, notice that in verse 16 of the prophecy it says, *"and thine house and thy kingdom shall be established forever."* Was the prophet referring to a physical house, or is it more reasonable that he's using the term house the same way the words descendants, or dynasty, or family are used? If this is the case, then verses 12 and 13 are referring to the Messiah as well as Solomon. Christ would be a descendant of David and sit on his throne. When Jesus asked the Pharisees whose son the Messiah would be, they responded that he would be the Son of David, referring to the prophecies in Psalm 132 and 2 Samuel 7. Jesus asked them why if the Messiah is the son of David, does David call Him Lord?[325] The Messiah is David's Lord even though He is his descendant in the same way that John testified that Christ came before him even though John was born first.

The genealogy of Jesus given in Matthew[326] is the descent of Joseph from David and Abraham, and although Joseph is only Jesus' stepfather, Jesus inherits from him. This gives Jesus the legal title to the throne of Israel of the kings descended from David. The genealogy of Jesus given in Luke[327] is the physical descent of Mary[328] from David, Abraham, and Adam, and gives Jesus the bloodline of David. Jesus is the seed of Mary.

---

[325] Mark 12:35-37; Psalms 110:1.
[326] Matthew 1:1-17.
[327] Luke 3:23-38.
[328] Jamieson, Fausset, and Brown and Matthew Henry's Commentaries on Luke 3:23-38.

There is one final note about this prophecy that should be mentioned. The prophecy says that the throne of David would be established forever. The Pharisees, when they condemned Jesus before Pilate, cried out, *"We have no king but Caesar."*[329] Thereafter, there has been no king in Israel for over 2,000 years. The throne of David is in abeyance awaiting the future reign of the Messiah.

In his trial before the Jewish Sanhedrin Jesus stated that he was the Messiah, the Son of God. Psalm 2 records a conversation between God and His Son. The people of the earth would rebel against God and seek to throw off His restraints. It says that God would laugh at them and tell them that He has set His King on the throne of Zion. God says, *"Yet have I set my king upon my holy hill of Zion."*[330]

The point of view changes and the Son of God relates what God has said to him:

> *I will declare the decree: the Lord hath said unto me, Thou art my Son; this day have I begotten thee. Ask of me, and I shall give thee the heathen for thine inheritance, and the uttermost parts of the earth for thy possession. Thou shalt break them with a rod of iron; thou shalt dash them in pieces like a potter's vessel. (Psalms 2:7-9 KJV)*

The Messiah will sit as king and rule over all the earth. God told the Messiah, *"This day have I begotten thee."* God is not saying that he created the Messiah on that day. He is saying that He is declaring that the Messiah is His Son and heir, the owner and ruler of creation. The New Testament reports that Jesus is the *"only begotten of the Father."*[331] Paul refers back to Psalm 2 to tell people

---

[329] John 19:15.
[330] Psalms 2:6 KJV.
[331] John 1:14,8, 3:16.

that Jesus is the *"only begotten son of God."*[332] John again referred to Jesus as the *"only begotten son of God"* in his epistle.[333] Over the years, a number of heresies have been promulgated that Jesus Christ was created, based upon these scriptures, but God Himself testifies that the Messiah is God, and therefore the word begotten cannot be used to mean created.

The deity of Christ is confirmed in the prophecy of his birth in the book of Isaiah:

> *Therefore the Lord himself shall give you a sign; behold, a virgin shall conceive, and bear a son, and shall call his name Immanuel.* (Isaiah 7:14 KJV)

The name *"Immanuel"* means "God with us."[334] The deity of the Messiah is again confirmed in another of Isaiah's prophecies:

> *For unto us a child is born, unto us a son is given: and the government shall be upon his shoulder: and his name shall be called Wonderful, Counsellor, the mighty God, the everlasting Father, the Prince of Peace. Of the increase of his government and peace there shall be no end, upon the throne of David, and upon his kingdom, to order it, and to establish it with judgment and with justice from henceforth even for ever. The zeal of the Lord of hosts will perform this.* (Isaiah 9:6-7 KJV)

Isaiah says that the Messiah's name would be, *"the mighty God,"* and *"the everlasting Father."* It was reiterated in this prophecy that the Messiah would be God Himself. Also, it is confirmed in

---

[332] Acts 13:33.

[333] 1 John 4:9.

[334] Strong's number h6005, *Immanuel*.

this prophecy that the Messiah would be the one to occupy the throne of David.

The fact of the deity of the Messiah is so important that God again confirms it in in His prophecy to Micah of the birth of the Messiah, the King:

> *But thou, Bethlehem Ephratah, though thou be little among the thousands of Judah, yet out of thee shall he come forth unto me that is to be ruler in Israel; whose goings forth have been from of old, from everlasting.* (Micah 5:2 KJV)

The same prophecy that the scribes used to tell King Herod where the Messiah would be born, confirms that he has existed eternally, an attribute that only belongs to God, the eternally self-existent One.

The writer of Psalm 45, speaking of the Messiah in a vision of him says that he is more handsome than the sons of man, and says that God has blessed him forever:

> *Thou art fairer than the children of men: grace is poured into thy lips: therefore God hath blessed thee for ever.* (Psalms 45:2 KJV)

The writer then calls on the Messiah to take up his power and glory, and rule over his kingdom and slay his enemies:

> *Gird thy sword upon thy thigh, O most mighty, with thy glory and thy majesty. And in thy majesty ride prosperously because of truth and meekness and righteousness; and thy right hand shall teach thee terrible things. Thine arrows are sharp in the heart of the king's enemies; whereby the people fall under thee.* (Psalms 45:3-5 KJV)

Still speaking of the Messiah, the Psalmist addresses Him as God and says that his throne, his kingdom, will last forever:

> *Thy throne, O God, is for ever and ever: the sceptre of thy kingdom is a right sceptre. Thou lovest righteousness, and hatest wickedness: therefore God, thy God, hath anointed thee with the oil of gladness above thy fellows.* (Psalms 45:6-7 KJV)

Because the Messiah loves righteousness and hates wickedness, God has anointed him with the oil of gladness more than anyone else. The preceding two verses of the Psalm say that the Messiah is God and that he is a person distinct from God.[335]

Further down in the Psalm, the Psalmist commands the queen betrothed to the Messiah to worship him:

> *Hearken, O daughter, and consider, and incline thine ear; forget also thine own people, and thy father's house; so shall the king greatly desire thy beauty: for he is thy Lord; and worship thou him.* (Psalms 45:10-11 KJV)

The Psalmist is saying that it is proper to worship the Messiah, who is the king, because he is Lord and God. God promises to exalt the name of the Messiah forever.[336]

Moving on to the prophecies of the Messiah in Daniel, Daniel says that the kingdom that God creates, the kingdom of the Messiah, will destroy all earthly kingdoms and grow to fill the whole earth:

---

[335] The interested reader can read more on the Christian doctrine that God and Christ are both God yet distinct persons at https://www.britannica.com/topic/homoousios

[336] Psalms 45:17.

86

Thou sawest till that a stone was cut out without hands, which smote the image upon his feet that were of iron and clay, and brake them to pieces. Then was the iron, the clay, the brass, the silver, and the gold, broken to pieces together, and became like the chaff of the summer threshingfloors; and the wind carried them away, that no place was found for them: and the stone that smote the image became a great mountain, and filled the whole earth. ... And in the days of these kings shall the God of heaven set up a kingdom, which shall never be destroyed: and the kingdom shall not be left to other people, but it shall break in pieces and consume all these kingdoms, and it shall stand for ever. (Daniel 2:34-35,44 KJV)

The Son of Man, the Messiah, appears before God and is given a kingdom that will last forever. He will sit on the throne of God and have dominion over all nations forever:

I saw in the night visions, and, behold, one like the Son of man came with the clouds of heaven, and came to the Ancient of days, and they brought him near before him. And there was given him dominion, and glory, and a kingdom, that all people, nations, and languages, should serve him: his dominion is an everlasting dominion, which shall not pass away, and his kingdom that which shall not be destroyed. (Daniel 7:13-14 KJV)

Jesus Christ claimed that he is the Messiah, the Son of Man, and the Son of God. He claimed his lordship and his kingship before the disciples, the Jewish Sanhedrin, and Pilate's tribunal. He was crucified under the title, *"The King of the Jews."* The image of Christ as the King in the Gospels is the image of the Messiah as the King in the scriptures of the Old Testament.

5.4.1.2 The Prophet of God

Not only does the Messiah sit in the office of king, but also the Messiah sits in the office of the prophet of God. The Apostle John tells us that Jesus is the actual word of God himself:

> *In the beginning was the Word, and the Word was with God, and the Word was God. The same was in the beginning with God. All things were made by him; and without him was not any thing made that was made. In him was life; and the life was the light of men ... And the Word was made flesh, and dwelt among us, (and we beheld his glory, the glory as of the only begotten of the Father,) full of grace and truth.* (John 1:1-4,14 KJV)

At the end of the forty years of wandering in the desert, Israel was poised to cross over the river Jordan into the Promised Land. The original generation of Israel that God led out of Egypt had gathered at the foot of Mount Sinai and heard the voice of God speak His commandments to them. When they rebelled and refused to enter into the Promised Land, God swore in His wrath that they would all die in the desert, and that He would lead their children into the Promised Land, the land they had rejected.[337] Moses recounted all of the law to the next generation of Israel on the opposite side of the Jordan River before they were to enter the Promised Land.

God promised that He was going to send a "Prophet" to the

---

[337] Numbers 14:31-33.

children of Israel and whoever wouldn't listen to Him would be judged:

> *I will raise them up a Prophet from among their*
> *brethren, like unto thee, and will put my words in*
> *his mouth; and he shall speak unto them all that I*
> *shall command him. And it shall come to pass, that*
> *whosoever will not hearken unto my words which*
> *he shall speak in my name, I will require it of him.*
> (Deuteronomy 18:18-19 KJV)

Notice that the word *"Prophet"* is capitalized, meaning that he was speaking of one particular prophet, not prophets in general. Now some people would say that the capitalization of the word Prophet in this scripture is an addition made by the translators of *The Bible*. But all of Israel understood this to be a prophecy of the Messiah, and they referred to it when they questioned John the Baptist about whether he was the Prophet, i.e., the Messiah.[338]

God revealed to Moses that the Prophet would speak the words of God. God said that whoever wouldn't listen to the words of God spoken by the Prophet, would be found guilty by God. Jesus reiterated what God told Moses:

> *And if any man hear my words, and believe not, I*
> *judge him not: for I came not to judge the world, but*
> *to save the world. He that rejecteth me, and receiveth*
> *not my words, hath one that judgeth him: the word*
> *that I have spoken, the same shall judge him in the*
> *last day. For I have not spoken of myself; but the*
> *Father which sent me, he gave me a commandment,*
> *what I should say, and what I should speak.* (John
> 12:47-50 KJV)

---

[338] John 1:19-23.

Jesus is the Prophet spoken of by Moses.

5.4.1.3 The Priest of God

Not only would the Messiah be king and prophet, but also He would be a priest forever after the order of Melchizedek. Jesus confirmed that Psalm 110 was describing the Messiah when He quoted it while questioning the Pharisees.[339] God swore an oath to confirm that the Messiah would be a priest forever:

> *The Lord hath sworn, and will not repent, Thou art a priest for ever after the order of Melchizedek.* (Psalms 110:4 KJV)

The Levitical priesthood had specific duties called out by God in the carrying out of their office as priests. They were to approach God in the knowledge of His Holiness. They were to glorify God before the people. When speaking of the death of Nadab and Abihu who were burnt up when they offered strange fire before God, God told Moses:

> *And Moses said to Aaron, "This is what the Lord spoke, saying: 'By those who come near Me I must be regarded as holy; and before all the people I must be glorified.'" So Aaron held his peace.* (Leviticus 10:3 NKJV)

Every priest in the Old Testament was under the same obligation, to approach the Lord God in the knowledge of His Holiness, and to glorify the Lord before all of the people that they represented. Priests were to fear the Lord and have the law of truth in their mouths. By their fear of God, their obedience to Him, and

---

[339] Mark 12:35-37.

having the word of truth in their mouths they would turn many people away from sin and iniquity and turn them to the Lord.[340]

The Messiah would be a priest forever, having the law of truth in his mouth. He would be the messenger of the Lord, the messenger of the new covenant of forgiveness from God. By His fear of God, by His obedience, and by the word of truth, He would turn many from their sin and wash them of their iniquity:

> *Behold, I will send my messenger, and he shall prepare the way before me: and the Lord, whom ye seek, shall suddenly come to his temple, even the messenger of the covenant, whom ye delight in: behold, he shall come, saith the Lord of hosts. But who may abide the day of his coming? And who shall stand when he appeareth? For he is like a refiner's fire, and like fullers' soap.* (Malachi 3:1-2 KJV)

The Messiah would be like a refiner's fire, removing the impurities in people, and leaving what was valuable.[341] John the Baptist, when witnessing of the Messiah to the Pharisees, confirmed the prophecy of Malachi, and said that the Messiah was the one that would baptize people with fire.[342]

The Messiah, the messenger of the covenant, would be like a powerful soap cleansing people of sin, washing the stain away. God promised people that He was going to provide a washing for sin:

> *Come now, and let us reason together, saith the Lord: though your sins be as scarlet, they shall be as white as snow; though they be red like crimson, they shall be as wool.* (Isaiah 1:18 KJV)

---

[340] Malachi 2:5-7.

[341] 1 Peter 1:7.

[342] Luke 3:16-17.

The writer of Hebrews applies the prophecies of the priesthood of the Messiah to Jesus and calls him the Son of God when he says:

> *So also Christ did not glorify Himself to become High Priest, but it was He who said to Him: "You are My Son, today I have begotten You." As He also says in another place: "You are a priest forever according to the order of Melchizedek"; who, in the days of His flesh, when He had offered up prayers and supplications, with vehement cries and tears to Him who was able to save Him from death, and was heard because of His godly fear, though He was a Son, yet He learned obedience by the things which He suffered. And having been perfected, He became the author of eternal salvation to all who obey Him, called by God as High Priest "according to the order of Melchizedek."* (Hebrews 5:5-10 NKJV)

Jesus is the high priest who offered Himself as the sacrifice for the sin of men. John called Jesus the Lamb of God, the sacrifice whose blood would be sprinkled on the Mercy Seat. All of the previous sacrifices of the Levitical priesthood were really a presaging of the work of Jesus; His blood would be sprinkled on the mercy seat for the sin of mankind:

> *For even the Son of man came not to be ministered unto, but to minister, and to give his life a ransom for many.* (Mark 10:45 KJV)

> *I am the living bread which came down from heaven: if any man eat of this bread, he shall live for ever: and the bread that I will give is my flesh, which I will give for the life of the world.* (John 6:51 KJV)

The author of the book of Hebrews tells us that Jesus entered into the Most Holy Place with His own blood to make a way for us to be forgiven by God. It was only the High Priest who could offer the sacrifice for sin in the Old Testament. Jesus was made the High Priest by God and offered Himself in our place. The resurrection of Christ shows that God has accepted his offering:

> *But Christ being come an high priest of good things to come, by a greater and more perfect tabernacle, not made with hands, that is to say, not of this building; neither by the blood of goats and calves, but by his own blood he entered in once into the holy place, having obtained eternal redemption for us. For if the blood of bulls and of goats, and the ashes of an heifer sprinkling the unclean, sanctifieth to the purifying of the flesh: How much more shall the blood of Christ, who through the eternal Spirit offered himself without spot to God, purge your conscience from dead works to serve the living God? And for this cause he is the mediator of the new testament, that by means of death, for the redemption of the transgressions that were under the first testament, they which are called might receive the promise of eternal inheritance.* (Hebrews 9:11-15 KJV)

Jesus was spotless, without sin, when He offered himself to God.

When the priesthood of the Messiah is understood it gives insight into a significant event during the trial of Jesus before the Sanhedrin.[343] During His trial, Jesus, the Messiah, stood before the High Priest, Caiaphas. Caiaphas was wearing the robe of His office as High Priest. In the Old Testament, God had commanded

---

[343] Matthew 26:62-65.

Moses to make the High Priest's robe of the ephod out of one piece of cloth and sew a binding around the edge of the hole where it went over the head of the High Priest so that it would not tear.[344] During the trial, Caiaphas put Jesus under oath and asked Him if He were the Christ, the Son of the Living God? Jesus said that He was and upon hearing His answer, Caiaphas tore the robe of his office in outrage. The office of the High Priest of the Levitical priesthood ended at that moment in the presence of the eternal priest of Melchizedek, Jesus Christ, the Messiah. It's significant that Jesus also wore a woven one-piece robe without seams, which the executioners gambled for when they crucified Him because they didn't want to tear it.[345]

Now some people might say that the High Priest only wore his robe of office when he was ministering in the temple. But the custom of the people of Israel during those days was to rend or tear their clothes to express their grief when someone from their family died. However, the high priest was not to engage in this practice:

> And he that is the high priest among his brethren, upon whose head the anointing oil was poured, and that is consecrated to put on the garments, shall not uncover his head, nor rend his clothes; (Leviticus 21:10 KJV)

God has said that the Messiah would be a priest forever after the order of Melchizedek, implying an end to the Levitical priesthood.[346] This was one of the reasons that the Jewish scribes and priests rejected Jesus. They understood that if Jesus were the Messiah as He testified, their office as priests would be ended. The priests, the sons of Aaron, would no longer sit in their positions

---

[344] Exodus 28:31-32.

[345] John 19:23-24.

[346] Psalms 110:4.

of authority, ruling all life in Israel. They would be like everyone else needing to humble themselves before the Messiah and entreat Him to intercede for them before God. This was intolerable to them. They tried to hold onto their office as priests, but their own High Priest, Caiaphas, had torn it from their hands. Caiaphas' actions were an unintentional acknowledgment of the ending of the Levitical priesthood in the presence of the priesthood of Christ, and the tearing of the curtain in the temple was God's judgment that the Levitical priesthood was ended.[347]

5.4.2 Prophecies of the First Coming of the Messiah

The picture of the Messiah painted by God in the Old Testament included many details to authenticate His identity when He came. God ensured that no one could claim the identity of the Messiah except the Son of God. The prophecies are so many, so varied, and so detailed, that no one could mistake the evidence of God for the identification of the Messiah when He came.

Joseph prophesied that the Messiah would be born of the tribe of Judah.[348] David was of the tribe of Judah and the Messiah would be called the Son of David.[349] David came from the city of Bethlehem, Judah.[350] The Messiah would be born in Bethlehem, in the city of David.[351]

Isaiah prophesied that the Messiah would be born of a virgin and would be named Immanuel, God With Us:

> *Therefore the Lord himself shall give you a sign; behold, a virgin shall conceive, and bear a son, and shall call his name Immanuel.* (Isaiah 7:14 KJV)

---

[347] Mark 15:38.
[348] Genesis 49:10.
[349] 2 Samuel 7:12-13,16; Psalms 132:11.
[350] Ruth 1:1, 4:11-12, 4:18-22.
[351] Micah 5:2.

Many people have argued against this prophecy, saying that *The Bible* translators mistranslated the word used for virgin, *alma*, in the prophecy. Strong's Concordance (h5959) translates the word as *lass, damsel, maid,* or *virgin,* all descriptions of a young woman before maturity. The prophecy was given to King Ahaz of Judah as a supernatural sign of the Lord. What kind of supernatural sign would it be if it was just a prophecy that a woman would get pregnant?

The people who deny that this prophecy is about the virgin birth of Christ say that further on in the prophecy in verse 16 it says that before the child is old enough to refuse evil and choose good, the two kings fighting against King Ahaz would be forsaken, implying that the child would be born during the days of King Ahaz. Even though there is not a specific answer to this objection, many times the prophecies of God in the Old Testament have more than one fulfillment, and this might be the case here.

However, the reason this prophecy can be trusted that it is about the virgin birth of the Messiah is that the Apostle Matthew, under the inspiration of the Holy Spirit, tells us that the birth of Christ is the fulfillment of this prophecy. Matthew reports the words of the angel of the Lord to Joseph, the husband of Mary:

> *Then Joseph her husband, being a just man, and not willing to make her a public example, was minded to put her away privily. But while he thought on these things, behold, the angel of the Lord appeared unto him in a dream, saying, Joseph, thou son of David, fear not to take unto thee Mary thy wife: for that which is conceived in her is of the Holy Ghost. And she shall bring forth a son, and thou shalt call his name Jesus: for he shall save his people from their sins. Now all this was done, that it might be fulfilled which was spoken of the Lord by the prophet, saying, behold, a virgin shall be with child, and shall bring*

forth a son, and they shall call his name Emmanuel, which being interpreted is, God with us. (Matthew 2:19-23 KJV)

Other than God Himself, there are only two people in a position to know about the virgin birth of Christ, and they are Joseph, and Mary. The knowledge of God's testimony to Joseph and Mary, and the knowledge of the virgin birth, was familiar to the apostles and disciples. It either came from their eyewitness testimony, or the Holy Spirit revealed it to the writers of the New Testament. When confronting Jesus, the Pharisees implied that they knew the prophecy of the virgin birth and further implied that Jesus had been born of fornication.[352]

The fitness of the Messiah to be a sacrifice for sin depended on him being sinless. If the Christ had been born of a human father, then his death on the cross could not have been a substitute for anyone else; it would have only been in payment for his own sins. But Jesus Christ is the Son of God, not of man, and is therefore sinless. He challenged the Pharisees to witness to any sin in him.[353]

The writer of Hebrews continues in the same theme and confirms the sinlessness of Christ:

> *Seeing then that we have a great high priest, that is passed into the heavens, Jesus the Son of God, let us hold fast our profession. For we have not an high priest which cannot be touched with the feeling of our infirmities; but was in all points tempted like as we are, yet without sin. (Hebrews 4:14-15 KJV)*

The Old Testament prophesied that God would call his son out of Egypt:

---

[352] John 8:41.
[353] John 8:46.

> *When Israel was a child, then I loved him, and called*
> *my son out of Egypt.* (Hosea 11:1 KJV)

Earlier when talking about the virgin birth of the Messiah, it was said that many times the prophecies of God have more than one fulfillment. At the time of the Exodus, God called Israel out of Egypt. But Matthew tells us that this prophecy had its fulfillment in the life of Christ; it was a specific prophecy about the Messiah.

God told Joseph to take Mary and Jesus and flee to Egypt to escape the persecution of King Herod:

> *And when they were departed, behold, the angel of*
> *the Lord appeareth to Joseph in a dream, saying, arise,*
> *and take the young child and his mother, and flee into*
> *Egypt, and be thou there until I bring thee word: for*
> *Herod will seek the young child to destroy him. When*
> *he arose, he took the young child and his mother by*
> *night, and departed into Egypt: and was there until*
> *the death of Herod: that it might be fulfilled which*
> *was spoken of the Lord by the prophet, saying, out of*
> *Egypt have I called my son.* (Matthew 2:13-15 KJV)

Once Herod died, God called Joseph and Mary to return:

> *But when Herod was dead, behold, an angel of the*
> *Lord appeareth in a dream to Joseph in Egypt, saying,*
> *arise, and take the young child and his mother, and go*
> *into the land of Israel: for they are dead which sought*
> *the young child's life. And he arose, and took the*
> *young child and his mother, and came into the land*
> *of Israel.* (Matthew 2:19-21 KJV)

The Old Testament prophesied that the Messiah would minister in the region of Galilee. Galilee was in the area of the ten northern tribes of Israel which were conquered by the Assyrians in ~720 BC and all of the people of the ten tribes were dispersed to live among the peoples of other nations. At the same time the Assyrians carried the Israelites away captive, they brought people in from other lands to settle the regions formerly occupied by Israel.[354] These peoples became known as Samaritans, having been resettled in Samaria. The tribes of Zebulun and Naphtali were among the ten northern tribes thrown out of their land. But God promised that the Messiah would come and shine a great light on the region:

> *Nevertheless the dimness shall not be such as was in her vexation, when at the first he lightly afflicted the land of Zebulun and the land of Naphtali, and afterward did more grievously afflict her by the way of the sea, beyond Jordan, in Galilee of the nations. The people that walked in darkness have seen a great light: they that dwell in the land of the shadow of death, upon them hath the light shined.* (Isaiah 9:1-2 KJV)

It is interesting that the Pharisees sent guards to arrest Jesus and they couldn't. The people were arguing over whether Jesus was the Christ and concerning his ministry originating in Galilee:

> *Many of the people therefore, when they heard this saying, said, of a truth this is the Prophet. Others said, this is the Christ. But some said, shall Christ come out of Galilee? Hath not the scripture said, that Christ cometh of the seed of David, and out of the town of Bethlehem, where David was? So there was a division among the people because of him.* (John 7:40-43 KJV)

---

[354] 2 Kings 17:23-24.

When the guards returned without Jesus under arrest, having been deterred because of the opinion of the people, the rulers castigated the guards and said the people were accursed. Nicodemus replied that they shouldn't judge Christ until they heard him:

> *Doth our law judge any man, before it hear him, and*
> *know what he doeth? They answered and said unto*
> *him, art thou also of Galilee? Search, and look: for*
> *out of Galilee ariseth no prophet.* (John 7:51-52 KJV)

Again the Pharisees and leaders of the Sanhedrin demonstrated their ignorance of the very scriptures they were supposed to know. They said, "*For out of Galilee ariseth no prophet.*" They had forgotten about the prophet Jonah. He was the son of Amitai.[355] Amitai and Jonah resided in Gath-Hepher,[356] a town in Galilee.[357] Jesus had told the Pharisees that the sign of Jonah would be the only sign they would be given to authenticate that Jesus was the Christ, but they never investigated Jonah. The Pharisees and the rulers of Israel ignored Jonah, Micah, and any other prophets that would prove the identity of Jesus. They weren't interested. Jesus was a threat to them and they weren't going to rest until they disposed of that threat.

Zechariah prophesied during the time of the return of the Jews from Babylon when they were rebuilding the temple. There are a number of prophecies about the Messiah contained in the book of Zechariah. Zechariah told Jerusalem to shout and rejoice because their king would come to them riding on a donkey:

> *Rejoice greatly, O daughter of Zion; shout, O daughter*
> *of Jerusalem: behold, thy King cometh unto thee: he*

---

[355] Jonah 1:1.

[356] 2 Kings 14:25.

[357] *https://en.wikipedia.org/wiki/Gath-hepher*

*is just, and having salvation; lowly, and riding upon
an ass, and upon a colt the foal of an ass.* (Zechariah
9:9 KJV)

The king would enter into Jerusalem bringing salvation to the
people. On Palm Sunday, the week before Jesus was crucified, he
entered into Jerusalem riding on a donkey. This is the only time
that Jesus is seen riding any animal. The entire three years of his
ministry, he and his disciples walked everywhere.

The Apostle John tells us that Jesus did this in fulfillment of
Zechariah's prophecy:

> *On the next day much people that were come to
> the feast, when they heard that Jesus was coming to
> Jerusalem, took branches of palm trees, and went
> forth to meet him, and cried, Hosanna: blessed is
> the King of Israel that cometh in the name of the
> Lord. And Jesus, when he had found a young ass,
> sat thereon; as it is written, fear not, daughter of
> Sion: behold, thy King cometh, sitting on an ass's colt.
> These things understood not his disciples at the first:
> but when Jesus was glorified, then remembered they
> that these things were written of him, and that they
> had done these things unto him.* (John 12:12-16 KJV)

Everywhere that Jesus went there was a mix of people who
believed that he was the promised Messiah and other people who
denied that he was the Christ. On Palm Sunday when he entered
Jerusalem, the people who believed that he was the Messiah
reacted to his entrance with joy and praise, confirming that Jesus
was the Messiah, the King of Israel, and worshipped him as he

entered. The Pharisees denied that Jesus was from God and called on Jesus to rebuke his disciples.[358]

The rulers of Israel rejected Jesus' testimony that he was the Christ. They rejected God's confirmation of Jesus testimony by the miracles that he worked. But God had given prophecies that the people and rulers of Israel would reject the Messiah. The prophet Isaiah tells us that the Messiah would be a man of sorrows and rejected by men:

> *He is despised and rejected of men; a man of sorrows, and acquainted with grief: and we hid as it were our faces from him; he was despised, and we esteemed him not. (Isaiah 53:3 KJV)*

And the unattributed writer of Psalm 118 says:

> *The stone which the builders refused is become the head stone of the corner. This is the Lord's doing; it is marvellous in our eyes. (Psalms 118:22-23 KJV)*

At the opposition of the scribes and Pharisees to Jesus, He told the parable of the owner of a vineyard who rented it to men who refused to give the owner his share of the fruit of the vineyard. The evil men went so far as to kill the son of the owner and take the vineyard for themselves.[359] The Pharisees knew that the parable was about them, but instead of repenting of their opposition to Him, they hardened themselves in their rejection of Him.

Jesus promised that because of their opposition to Christ, the kingdom would be taken from them and given to others who would bring forth fruit to God:

---

[358] Luke 19:38-40.
[359] Matthew 21:33-41.

Jesus saith unto them, did ye never read in the scriptures, the stone which the builders rejected, the same is become the head of the corner: this is the Lord's doing, and it is marvellous in our eyes? Therefore say I unto you, the kingdom of God shall be taken from you, and given to a nation bringing forth the fruits thereof. And whosoever shall fall on this stone shall be broken: but on whomsoever it shall fall, it will grind him to powder. And when the chief priests and Pharisees had heard his parables, they perceived that he spake of them. (Matthew 21:42-45 KJV)

The rulers of Israel rejected Christ right up until the end. They denied their king in front of Pilate, the Roman Governor:

And it was the preparation of the passover, and about the sixth hour: and he saith unto the Jews, Behold your King! But they cried out, away with him, away with him, crucify him. Pilate saith unto them, shall I crucify your King? The chief priests answered, we have no king but Caesar. (John 19:14-15 KJV)

In Daniel's seventy weeks of years prophecy about the coming of the Messiah, it specifically says that Messiah would be cut-off at an exact time:

Know therefore and understand, that from the going forth of the commandment to restore and to build Jerusalem unto the Messiah the Prince shall be seven weeks, and threescore and two weeks: the street shall be built again, and the wall, even in troublous times. And after threescore and two weeks shall Messiah be cut off, but not for himself: and the people of the prince that shall come shall destroy the city and

> *the sanctuary; and the end thereof shall be with a*
> *flood, and unto the end of the war desolations are*
> *determined.* (Daniel 9:25-26 KJV)

Again, referring to the book, *The Coming Prince,* by Sir Robert Anderson, the crucifixion of Christ was at the exact time spoken of in the prophecy of Daniel. The scribes and Pharisees demonstrated their knowledge of the prophecy when they questioned John the Baptist, but showed their ignorance of the meaning of it.

Not only was the Messiah to be rejected by the rulers and leaders of his nation, but also His zeal for the Lord of Hosts would consume Him. His own family would be estranged from Him:

> *Because for thy sake I have borne reproach; shame*
> *hath covered my face. I am become a stranger unto*
> *my brethren, and an alien unto my mother's children.*
> *For the zeal of thine house hath eaten me up; and the*
> *reproaches of them that reproached thee are fallen*
> *upon me.* (Psalms 69:7-9 KJV)

The reproaches of the people towards God would fall on the Messiah. This prophecy was fulfilled in two different parts in the life of Christ. At the time of His first cleansing of the temple, He exhibited His zeal for his Father's house:

> *And the Jews' passover was at hand, and Jesus went*
> *up to Jerusalem, and found in the temple those that*
> *sold oxen and sheep and doves, and the changers of*
> *money sitting: and when he had made a scourge of*
> *small cords, he drove them all out of the temple, and*
> *the sheep, and the oxen; and poured out the changers'*
> *money, and overthrew the tables; and said unto them*
> *that sold doves, take these things hence; make not*
> *my Father's house an house of merchandise. And his*

disciples remembered that it was written, the zeal of thine house hath eaten me up. (John 2:13-17 KJV)

Later, the apostle John confirms that even Christ's own brothers didn't believe in Him until after the resurrection:

Now the Jews' Feast of Tabernacles was at hand. His brothers therefore said to Him, "Depart from here and go into Judea, that Your disciples also may see the works that You are doing. For no one does anything in secret while he himself seeks to be known openly. If You do these things, show Yourself to the world." For even His brothers did not believe in Him. (John 7:2-5 NKJV)

The Old Testament tells us in multiple places that His friend would betray the Messiah. The friend of the Messiah was the one who had gone to the temple to worship with Him:

For it was not an enemy that reproached me; then I could have borne it: neither was it he that hated me that did magnify himself against me; then I would have hid myself from him: but it was thou, a man mine equal, my guide, and mine acquaintance. We took sweet counsel together, and walked unto the house of God in company. (Psalms 55:12-14 KJV)

They had enjoyed sweet fellowship together before his betrayal. He turned his back on the Messiah and lifted up his heal against him:

Yea, mine own familiar friend, in whom I trusted, which did eat of my bread, hath lifted up his heel against me. (Psalms 41:9 KJV)

Jesus Himself claimed Judas Iscariot fulfilled this scripture in His betrayal. Judas was the one who lifted up his heel against Christ:

> *I speak not of you all: I know whom I have chosen: but that the scripture may be fulfilled, He that eateth bread with me hath lifted up his heel against me ... Jesus answered, He it is, to whom I shall give a sop, when I have dipped it. And when he had dipped the sop, he gave it to Judas Iscariot, the son of Simon.* (John 13:18, 26)

Judas Iscariot was an apostle chosen by Jesus, who walked with Him the entire three years of His ministry. He listened to Jesus' teachings. He witnessed Jesus' miracles. He enjoyed the fellowship of Jesus. Jesus looked on Judas as His friend, even though he knew that Judas was going to betray him.[360]

Even after Judas betrayed him, Jesus still called him his friend:

> *And while he yet spake, lo, Judas, one of the twelve, came, and with him a great multitude with swords and staves, from the chief priests and elders of the people. Now he that betrayed him gave them a sign, saying, whomsoever I shall kiss, that same is he: hold him fast. And forthwith he came to Jesus, and said, hail, master; and kissed him. And Jesus said unto him, Friend, wherefore art thou come? Then came they, and laid hands on Jesus, and took him.* (Matthew 26:47-50 KJV)

Many people don't understand how Judas could betray Jesus after having been with Him for the entire period of His ministry.

---

[360] John 6:70-71, 13:10-11; Luke 22:21.

Even after witnessing everything Jesus did during his three years of ministry, Judas didn't believe that Jesus was the promised Messiah. He gave evidence of this during the last supper. Jesus told the disciples that one of them would betray Him, and all of the disciples asked Jesus if they were the one:

> *And they were exceedingly sorrowful, and each of them began to say to Him, "Lord, is it I?" He answered and said, "He who dipped his hand with Me in the dish will betray Me. The Son of Man indeed goes just as it is written of Him, but woe to that man by whom the Son of Man is betrayed! It would have been good for that man if he had not been born." Then Judas, who was betraying Him, answered and said, "Rabbi, is it I?" He said to him, "You have said it."* (Matthew 26:22-25 NKJV)

Notice in the above passage that all of the disciples except Judas said, *"Lord is it I?"* But Judas says, *"Rabbi, is it I?"* The other disciples acknowledged that Jesus is their Lord, but Judas only acknowledges that Jesus is Rabbi, meaning Teacher. Jesus said to Judas that out of his own mouth he is condemned, *"You have said it."* Judas didn't believe that Jesus was the Christ.

John tells us also that Judas was a thief and would steal what was in the moneybag that he was in charge of.[361] Maybe Judas thought that since Christ had prophesied that he was going to die, he could take advantage of the situation and earn some money on the side? Maybe he rationalized that he wasn't really doing anything wrong since Christ had already foretold what was going to happen? The motives of Judas are not clear. But Jesus said that it would have been better if Judas had never been born.

Even though it was God's will that the Messiah die for the sins

---

[361] John 12:6.

of people, He still held the people responsible for the death of the Messiah accountable for their evil actions. Peter confirmed this in his Pentecost message to the people of Jerusalem:

> *Ye men of Israel, hear these words; Jesus of Nazareth, a man approved of God among you by miracles and wonders and signs, which God did by him in the midst of you, as ye yourselves also know: Him, being delivered by the determinate counsel and foreknowledge of God, ye have taken, and by wicked hands have crucified and slain: Whom God hath raised up, having loosed the pains of death: because it was not possible that he should be holden of it.* (Acts 2:22-24 KJV)

Jesus was betrayed by a friend in accord with prophecy. Not only did the Old Testament report that a friend would betray the Messiah, but it reported the exact amount of money that Judas would receive for his betrayal:

> *And I said unto them, If ye think good, give me my price; and if not, forbear. So they weighed for my price thirty pieces of silver. And the Lord said unto me, cast it unto the potter: a goodly price that I was prised at of them. And I took the thirty pieces of silver, and cast them to the potter in the house of the Lord.* (Zechariah 11:12-13 KJV)

Matthew tells us that Judas agreed to betray Christ for thirty pieces of silver:

> *Then one of the twelve, called Judas Iscariot, went unto the chief priests, and said unto them, what will ye give me, and I will deliver him unto you? And they*

*covenanted with him for thirty pieces of silver. And
from that time he sought opportunity to betray him.*
(Matthew 26:14-16 KJV)

Actually, the prophecy in the book of Zechariah has two parts,
first the price of thirty silver pieces is paid for the Messiah, and
then the silver is cast to the potter in the house of the Lord.

Matthew reported that when Judas understood that his
betrayal of Christ had condemned Him to death he went back
to the chief priests and scribes and returned the money to them
trying to atone for his actions. He confessed his sin and cast the
money on the floor of the temple:

> *Then Judas, which had betrayed him, when he saw
> that he was condemned, repented himself, and brought
> again the thirty pieces of silver to the chief priests and
> elders, saying, I have sinned in that I have betrayed
> the innocent blood. And they said, what is that to
> us? See thou to that. And he cast down the pieces
> of silver in the temple, and departed, and went and
> hanged himself. And the chief priests took the silver
> pieces, and said, it is not lawful for to put them into
> the treasury, because it is the price of blood. And they
> took counsel, and bought with them the potter's field,
> to bury strangers in.* (Matthew 27:3-7 KJV)

The priests took the money and gave it for the purchase of
the potter's field to bury the indigent in, so between Judas and the
priests both parts of the prophecy of Zechariah were fulfilled.[362]

Isaiah prophesied that the Messiah would be humiliated, spit
on, and beaten:

---

[362] See also Matthew 27:9-10; Jeremiah 32:6-9.

> *The Lord God hath opened mine ear, and I was not rebellious, neither turned away back. I gave my back to the smiters, and my cheeks to them that plucked off the hair: I hid not my face from shame and spitting. For the Lord God will help me; therefore shall I not be confounded: therefore have I set my face like a flint, and I know that I shall not be ashamed. (Isaiah 50:5-7 KJV)*

During the illegal trial on the night before His crucifixion, the members of the Sanhedrin struck Jesus, spit on Him, and reviled Him:

> *What think ye? They answered and said, He is guilty of death. Then did they spit in his face, and buffeted him; and others smote him with the palms of their hands, saying, prophesy unto us, thou Christ, who is he that smote thee? (Matthew 26:66-68 KJV)*

Jesus stoically accepted their abuse. In his prophecy, Isaiah says that the Messiah's face was set as flint, meaning He was determined to carry out the will of God no matter the shame that was associated with it. Jesus voluntarily laid down His life in obedience to God's will so that people might be saved from the wrath of God against sin.[363]

The author of Hebrews says that Jesus went to the cross, despising the shame, because of the joy that God set before Him, the joy of the salvation that Jesus was going to work for people by dying on the cross.[364]

The Old Testament tells us that the Messiah was going to be

---

[363] John 10:17.
[364] Hebrews 12:1-2.

wounded, bruised, and chastised for our sin, transgressions, and iniquities. He would receive stripes in our place:

> *But he was wounded for our transgressions, he was bruised for our iniquities: the chastisement of our peace was upon him; and with his stripes we are healed. All we like sheep have gone astray; we have turned every one to his own way; and the Lord hath laid on him the iniquity of us all.* (Isaiah 53:5-6 KJV)

Before Pontius Pilate crucified Christ, he had him flogged by the Roman guard:

> *Then released he Barabbas unto them: and when he had scourged Jesus, he delivered him to be crucified.* (Matthew 27:26 KJV)

Jesus told the disciples that His blood was going to be shed for the remission of sins. With the death of Jesus, His blood would be the promise of the new covenant, a promise of forgiveness from God for all those who put their faith in Christ:

> *And as they were eating, Jesus took bread, and blessed it, and brake it, and gave it to the disciples, and said, take, eat; this is my body. And he took the cup, and gave thanks, and gave it to them, saying, drink ye all of it; for this is my blood of the new testament, which is shed for many for the remission of sins.* (Matthew 26:26-28 KJV)

> *How God anointed Jesus of Nazareth with the Holy Ghost and with power: who went about doing good, and healing all that were oppressed of the devil; for God was with him. And we are witnesses of all things*

> *which he did both in the land of the Jews, and in Jerusalem; whom they slew and hanged on a tree: him God raised up the third day, and shewed him openly; not to all the people, but unto witnesses chosen before of God, even to us, who did eat and drink with him after he rose from the dead. And he commanded us to preach unto the people, and to testify that it is he which was ordained of God to be the Judge of quick and dead. To him give all the prophets witness, that through his name whosoever believeth in him shall receive remission of sins. (Acts 10:38-43 KJV)*

God gave many details of the crucifixion of the Messiah in the Old Testament. He told us that the Messiah would be given gall and vinegar:

> *Reproach hath broken my heart; and I am full of heaviness: and I looked for some to take pity, but there was none; and for comforters, but I found none. They gave me also gall for my meat; and in my thirst they gave me vinegar to drink. (Psalms 69:20-21 KJV)*

When wine has soured, it turns to vinegar. If you look up the word "*gall*"[365] in Strong's Concordance, it reports that it is most likely the poppy from which opium and morphine is derived. They offered gall to Jesus before they crucified Him to deaden the pain:

> *They gave him vinegar to drink mingled with gall: and when he had tasted thereof, he would not drink.* (Matthew 27:34 KJV)

---

[365] Strong's number h7219, '*rowsh*', a poisonous plant, probably the poppy...

The prophecies of the Old Testament state that the Messiah would be crucified and ridiculed on the cross. People would shake their heads and laugh at Him for trusting in God:

> *All they that see me laugh me to scorn: they shoot out the lip, they shake the head, saying, he trusted on the Lord that he would deliver him: let him deliver him, seeing he delighted in him. (Psalms 22:7-8 KJV)*

Under the inspiration of the Holy Spirit, David recorded the posture and exact words that the priests and leaders of Israel spoke to Christ when he was hanging on the cross:

> *And they that passed by reviled him, wagging their heads, and saying, thou that destroyest the temple, and buildest it in three days, save thyself. If thou be the Son of God, come down from the cross. – Likewise also the chief priests mocking him, with the scribes and elders, said, he saved others; himself he cannot save. If he be the King of Israel, let him now come down from the cross, and we will believe him. He trusted in God; let him deliver him now, if he will have him: for he said, I am the Son of God. (Matthew 27:39-43 KJV)*

Notice that the chief priests acknowledged that Jesus saved people. They acknowledged His miracles. They acknowledged that He claimed to be the Son of God. They understood His claim to be the Messiah, the King of Israel, but refused to acknowledge that Jesus was the Christ, no matter what evidence had been presented. One day they will stand before the judgment seat of God without excuse.

The Encyclopedia Britannica reports that the Persians,

Seleucids, Carthaginians, and Romans used crucifixion as early as the 6th century BC[366].

However, Psalm 22, with the description of the crucifixion, was penned by King David sometime around 1000 BC. Crucifixion was unknown as a form of capital punishment at the time David wrote the description of the crucifixion of the Messiah.

David gives a detailed description of the way in which the Messiah was crucified as well as the result of hanging on the cross:

> *I am poured out like water, and all my bones are out of joint: my heart is like wax; it is melted in the midst of my bowels. My strength is dried up like a potsherd; and my tongue cleaveth to my jaws; and thou hast brought me into the dust of death. For dogs have compassed me: the assembly of the wicked have inclosed me: they pierced my hands and my feet. I may tell all my bones: they look and stare upon me. They part my garments among them, and cast lots upon my vesture. (Psalms 22:14-18 KVJ)*

One result of crucifixion was that the joints in the shoulders would dislocate. The victims of crucifixion became incredibly thirsty as they died, and this is why, in fulfillment of prophecy, Jesus cried out from the cross, "*I thirst.*"[367] An assembly of the wicked surrounded Jesus, men Jesus had called the children of the devil.[368] They pierced His hands and His feet.

The Old Testament said that the lamb of the sacrifice had to be perfect, without blemish, and it was to have none of its bones broken.[369] Notice that the scripture from *Exodus* is referring to the Passover lamb. Not a bone of it was to be broken. John the

---

[366] http://www.britannica.com/topic/crucifixion-capital-punishment
[367] John 19:28.
[368] John 8:44.
[369] Exodus 12:46.

Baptist called Jesus, *"The Lamb of God."* He was the Passover Lamb. Because of that, the Messiah would not have a bone broken either. The two thieves crucified on either side of Jesus both had their legs broken by the Roman soldiers to hasten their death, but Jesus was already dead, so they didn't break His legs, but stabbed Him in His side to ensure that He was dead:

> *The Jews therefore, because it was the preparation, that the bodies should not remain upon the cross on the Sabbath day, (for that Sabbath day was an high day,) besought Pilate that their legs might be broken, and that they might be taken away. Then came the soldiers, and brake the legs of the first, and of the other which was crucified with him. But when they came to Jesus, and saw that he was dead already, they brake not his legs: but one of the soldiers with a spear pierced his side, and forthwith came there out blood and water.* (John 19:31-34 KJV)

God promised the Messiah that He would deliver Him out of all of His afflictions and not one of His bones would be broken:

> *Many are the afflictions of the righteous: but the Lord delivereth him out of them all. He keepeth all his bones: not one of them is broken.* (Psalms 34:19-20 KJV)

The book of Zechariah, which was written sometime in the 5th or 6th century BC, prophesied of the piercing of the Messiah:

> *And I will pour upon the house of David, and upon the inhabitants of Jerusalem, the spirit of grace and of supplications: and they shall look upon me whom they have pierced, and they shall mourn for him, as one*

> *mourneth for his only son, and shall be in bitterness*
> *for him, as one that is in bitterness for his firstborn.*
> (Zechariah 12:10 KJV)

Not only does this prophecy confirm the piercing of the Messiah, but also it states that at sometime in the future God will pour out on the Jews a spirit of grace and repentance. They will come to know that Jesus is the Messiah and will mourn over their refusal to believe in Him and the pain that has caused them down through history.

Zechariah also refers to the crucifixion of the Messiah when speaking of the wounds in His hands:

> *And one shall say unto him, what are these wounds in*
> *thine hands? Then he shall answer, those with which I*
> *was wounded in the house of my friends.* (Zechariah
> 13:6 KJV)

Isaiah prophesied that God would never forget His people. Everyone who is His, the Jews and the gentiles who come to salvation in Christ, He will remember forever:

> *Can a woman forget her sucking child, that she should*
> *not have compassion on the son of her womb? Yea,*
> *they may forget, yet will I not forget thee. Behold,*
> *I have graven thee upon the palms of my hands;*
> *thy walls are continually before me.* (Isaiah 49:15-
> 16 KJV)

Christ engraved our names on His hands when He was crucified for us. He was thinking of everyone who would be saved by His sacrifice while hanging on the cross.

In our quote from Psalm 22:14-18, it says, "*They part my garments among them, and cast lots upon my vesture.*" As was stated earlier when talking about the High Priest Caiaphas tearing his robe of office, Jesus was also wearing a one-piece robe without seam. It was customary for the Roman guards to divide up any belongings that a condemned man had among themselves. It was part of their wages as executioners. But they didn't want to ruin the robe that Jesus was wearing by tearing it into four parts, so they cast lots for it to see who should get it. God ensured that Jesus fulfilled the law even in the restriction that the robe of the High Priest shouldn't be torn:[370]

> *Then the soldiers, when they had crucified Jesus, took his garments, and made four parts, to every soldier a part; and also his coat: now the coat was without seam, woven from the top throughout. They said therefore among themselves, let us not rend it, but cast lots for it, whose it shall be: that the scripture might be fulfilled, which saith, they parted my raiment among them, and for my vesture they did cast lots. These things therefore the soldiers did. (John 19:23-24 KJV)*

The Messiah looked for someone to take pity on Him. He looked for people to comfort Him in the punishment He would suffer on the cross at God's behest, on behalf of the very people who were crucifying Him. But He found none. Instead, they gave Him vinegar and gall. David called out to God to punish the wicked who had done this.[371] But Jesus didn't call out an imprecatory prayer to God from the cross. Instead, He prayed that God would forgive those who crucified Him.[372]

---

[370] Exodus 28:31-32.
[371] Psalms 69:21-28.
[372] Luke 23:34.

The prophecies of the Old Testament stated that the Messiah would die with the wicked and be buried with the rich:

> *And he made his grave with the wicked, and with the rich in his death; because he had done no violence, neither was any deceit in his mouth.* (Isaiah 53:9 KJV)

Jesus was crucified between two thieves.[373] Not only that, but Jesus was crucified in the place of Barabbas:

> *And they cried out all at once, saying, away with this man, and release unto us Barabbas: (Who for a certain sedition made in the city, and for murder, was cast into prison.) … And he released unto them him that for sedition and murder was cast into prison, whom they had desired; but he delivered Jesus to their will.* (Luke 23:18-19,25 KJV)

Barabbas had committed murder in an insurrection and was in jail with the two thieves and would have been crucified with them if Jesus hadn't taken his place. It's a great picture for people. Everyone is under sentence of death, and Christ comes and takes their place.[374] Barabbas was set free and Christ was crucified. That is the gospel in a nutshell.

Joseph of Arimathea, a rich man, went to Pontius Pilate and asked permission to take the body of Jesus and bury it, and after ascertaining that Jesus was dead, Pilate released the body to him. Joseph and Nicodemus, a member of the Sanhedrin, took the body of Jesus, wrapped it in spices and burial clothes and laid it in a tomb that Joseph owned which had never had a body placed in it. David wrote that God would not let His Holy One see

---

[373] Matthew 27:38; Luke 23:32.
[374] John 3:36; Romans 6:23; et al.

corruption,[375] and Peter used that scripture when witnessing to the resurrection of Christ.[376] But God also made certain that not only did the body of Jesus not decay, but also it wasn't even placed in a tomb containing any decay. *"Neither wilt thou suffer thine Holy One to see corruption."* Jesus died between the wicked and His body was laid in a rich man's grave in accordance with prophecy.

So the Old Testament corroborates that Jesus is the Christ by the confirmation of the details of Jesus' life and ministry. Let's summarize what's been shown about the life and death of the Messiah during His first advent.

Jesus was the Son of David, of the tribe of Judah, and was born in Bethlehem exactly as prophesied for the Messiah. Jesus, the Lamb of God, was born of the Virgin Mary, and was without sin, a perfect sacrifice, divinely prepared for His role as the Messiah, the savior of mankind.

God called His Son out of Egypt, according to prophecy. God hid Jesus in Egypt until King Herod died to protect His life. And then God told Joseph and Mary to return, where they took up residence in Galilee. Jesus ministry was to be centered in Galilee and it was done exactly as prophecy had foretold.

Jesus presented himself as the King of Israel, entering into Jerusalem riding on a donkey, according to the scriptures. The rulers of Israel rejected Jesus just as had been foretold. Jesus' life was sacrificed. He was crucified on the cross at the exact time prophesied for the Messiah to be cut-off. He was betrayed by his friend, Judas Iscariot, according to prophecy, in fulfillment of the scriptures.[377]

Judas betrayed Christ for the exact amount, thirty silver pieces, that had been prophesied for the Messiah. Judas returned the blood money that he had received for betraying Jesus Christ. Judas

---

[375] Psalms 16:10.

[376] Acts 2:27.

[377] John 17:12.

cast the thirty pieces of silver to the floor of the temple, and the priests used it buy the potter's field exactly as scripture had foretold.

Prophecy told us that the Messiah would be spit on, humiliated, scourged and crucified in exact detail foretelling the experiences of Jesus in his trial before the Sanhedrin, in his judgment by Pilate, and in his death on the cross. The Messiah would be given vinegar and gall, exactly as occurred with Jesus.

The executioners of the Messiah would gamble for His clothing, because they didn't want to tear His one-piece robe, His robe of office as the high priest. The people watching his execution would laugh and jeer at him and taunt him using the very words written in the prophecy in Psalm 22.

Finally, Jesus was crucified between the wicked and buried in a rich man's grave, all details foretold about the Messiah.

The prophecies of the Old Testament corroborate the testimony of Jesus that He is the Christ.

5.4.3 The Resurrection of the Messiah

In the previous section, there were listed some of the many characteristics that could be used to authenticate that Jesus is the Messiah promised to Israel and all people. But there was one characteristic of His first coming that was left until now, and that is the resurrection of Christ. Earlier, proof was given of the resurrection of Christ. But the resurrection of the Messiah was prophesied in the Old Testament.

5.4.3.1 Prophecies of a General Resurrection in the Future

In many places, the Old Testament prophesies that there will be a resurrection of all men and women at some time in the future. God stopped Adam from continuing to eat from the Tree of Life when

He cast him out of the garden so that Adam wouldn't live forever in his sinful state, thereby revealing the possibility of eternal life.[378]

When questioned by the Sadducees who didn't believe in the resurrection, Jesus quoted God from His encounter with Moses at the burning bush. Jesus used God's statement to Moses:

> "*I am the God of thy father, the God of Abraham, the God of Isaac, and God of Jacob,*" (Exodus 3:6 KJV)

saying that God is God of the living, not of the dead, thereby confirming the resurrection.[379] If the dead weren't resurrected, God would have said, "I WAS the God of thy father, the God of Abraham, the God of Isaac, and God of Jacob."

In the book of Job, Job stated that one day in his resurrected body he would see his redeemer; he would see Christ:

> *For I know that my redeemer liveth, and that he shall stand at the latter day upon the earth: and though after my skin worms destroy this body, yet in my flesh shall I see God.* (Job 19:25-26 KJV)

Job confirmed that the resurrection is a physical, bodily resurrection, not just a spiritual after-life. Job would stand in his flesh and see God.

In the Psalms David said that "*God will redeem my soul from the power of the grave,*"[380] and stated "*The Lord commanded the blessing, even life forevermore,*"[381] confirming the resurrection.

Later, David confirms that God had commanded the blessing of eternal life:

---

[378] Genesis 3:22-24.
[379] Matthew 22:32.
[380] Psalms 49:15 KJV.
[381] Psalms 133:3 KJV.

> *It is like the dew of Hermon, descending upon the mountains of Zion; for there the Lord commanded the blessing—life forevermore.* (Psalms 133:3 NKJV)

The prophet Hosea quotes God as saying, "*I will ransom them from the power of the grave; I will redeem them from death,*"[382] a promise to resurrect people.

Jesus confirmed what the Old Testament states: that there will be a resurrection of the dead, some to eternal life and some to eternal damnation:

> *Marvel not at this: for the hour is coming, in the which all that are in the graves shall hear his voice, and shall come forth; they that have done good, unto the resurrection of life; and they that have done evil, unto the resurrection of damnation.* (John 5:28-29 KJV)

5.4.3.2 Prophecies of the Resurrection of the Messiah

What does the Old Testament have to say about the specific resurrection of the Messiah? David prophesies of the Messiah in Psalm 21 reporting that the Messiah asks life from God, and God gives Him life evermore:

> *He asked life of thee, and thou gavest it him, even length of days for ever and ever.* (Psalms 21:4 KJV)

Jesus indirectly referred to this passage in Psalms when he told the Pharisees that He has life in Himself and could give it to whomever He chose:

---

[382] Hosea 13:14 KVJ.

*Verily, verily, I say unto you, he that heareth my word,
and believeth on him that sent me, hath everlasting
life, and shall not come into condemnation; but is
passed from death unto life. Verily, verily, I say unto
you, the hour is coming, and now is, when the dead
shall hear the voice of the Son of God: and they that
hear shall live. For as the Father hath life in himself;
so hath he given to the Son to have life in himself;*
(John 5:24-26 KJV)

The apostle Peter confirmed that the resurrection of Christ
had been prophesied in the Old Testament.[383] He quoted David's
prophecy that God would resurrect him at the time of the end,
and that the Messiah would be resurrected even before His body
had time to decay:

*For thou wilt not leave my soul in hell; neither wilt
thou suffer thine Holy One to see corruption.* (Psalms
16:10 KJV)

The prophet Isaiah gives an implicit witness to the resurrection
of the Messiah in his description of Him:

*Yet it pleased the Lord to bruise him; he hath put him
to grief: when thou shalt make his soul an offering
for sin, he shall see his seed, he shall prolong his
days, and the pleasure of the Lord shall prosper in
his hand. He shall see of the travail of his soul, and
shall be satisfied: by his knowledge shall my righteous
servant justify many; for he shall bear their iniquities.
Therefore will I divide him a portion with the great,
and he shall divide the spoil with the strong; because*

---

[383] Acts 2:30-32.

> *he hath poured out his soul unto death: and he was*
> *numbered with the transgressors; and he bare the sin*
> *of many, and made intercession for the transgressors.*
> (Isaiah 53:10-12 KJV)

Notice in the above passage that it was the Lord's will to make the Messiah an offering for sin. Yet, in the very next phrase, it says the Messiah shall see His seed and He shall prolong His days. He would pour out His soul unto death, making intercession for sinners, yet He would see the fruit of His sacrifice in the children that He brought to God. Faith in the death of Christ as an offering for sin is at the root of being born again. Christians are the seeds of Christ, children born again to a living hope in Christ.[384] The salvation of people, their new birth in Christ, is the joy that God set before Christ that made Him willing to endure the shame of the cross.[385] The writer of Hebrews explains that the captain of salvation, the Christ, was made perfect by what He suffered.[386] He was made perfect in that His death on the cross proved His love for everyone, all those who were and are under sentence of death.[387]

The Old Testament confirmed that the Messiah would be resurrected, and corroborates the testimony of Christ and of God.

> *And the times of this ignorance God winked at; but*
> *now commandeth all men every where to repent:*
> *because he hath appointed a day, in the which he will*
> *judge the world in righteousness by that man whom he*
> *hath ordained; whereof he hath given assurance unto*
> *all men, in that he hath raised him from the dead.*
> (Acts 17:30-31 KJV)

---

[384] 1 Peter 1:3.
[385] Hebrews 12:1-2.
[386] Hebrews 2:10.
[387] Romans 5:8.

The resurrection of Jesus Christ was in accordance with prophecy and is the heart of the witness of Jesus Christ to God. Prophecy witnessed to Christ so that people would know Him when He came, and Christ witnessed to God, so they could be saved. It is an unbroken chain of testimony calling to everyone to repent and believe the Gospel.

6 The Doctrine of Christ

A ll four witnesses, John the Baptist, the miracles that Jesus performed, the testimony of God the Father, and the testimony of the Old Testament Scriptures have corroborated the testimony of Jesus. Jesus is the Christ, the Messiah, the anointed one of God, and His only begotten Son. He has been declared to be the Son of God by his resurrection from the dead. Everything that He said is true and trustworthy.

When Christ was teaching on the earth, He spoke in God's name, exercising God's authority, and it amazed people:

> And they were astonished at his doctrine: for he taught them as one that had authority, and not as the scribes. (Mark 1:22 KJV)

Knowing that Jesus is the only witness to God and heaven, what is the doctrine of Christ? Jesus testified that His doctrine is the doctrine of God:

> Jesus answered them and said, "My doctrine is not Mine, but His who sent Me. If anyone wills to do His will, he shall know concerning the doctrine, whether it is from God or whether I speak on My own authority. (John 7:16-17 NKJV)

Since Jesus has assured us that every word He spoke came from God,[388] His doctrine will never contradict anything that had already been written in the word of God, in the Scriptures. His doctrine is a confirmation of the written word of God. The Old Testament and the New Testament are one book, *The Bible*, and it is the word of God.

6.1 The Word of God is the Truth

The Bible has much to say about the word of God. The universe and all life were created by the word of God:

> *By the word of the Lord were the heavens made; and*
> *all the host of them by the breath of his mouth …*
> *For he spake, and it was done; he commanded, and*
> *it stood fast … The counsel of the Lord standeth*
> *for ever, the thoughts of his heart to all generations.*
> (Psalms 33:6,9,11 KJV)

Whatever God speaks is eternal:

> *For ever, O Lord, thy word is settled in heaven.*
> (Psalms 119:89 KJV)

Never will He contradict or countermand the word that he has spoken. Every promise of God is fixed, permanent, and eternal. He confirmed it in His promise to David to establish the throne of Christ forever.[389] He confirmed it in His promise to give Israel the land of Canaan. *The Bible* says that God remembers His covenant,

---

[388] John 12:50, 14:10.
[389] Psalms 89:34-37.

His promise, forever.[390] *The Bible* reiterates that every word of God is true and will last forever:

> *Thy word is true from the beginning: and every one of thy righteous judgments endureth for ever.* (Psalms 119:160 KJV)

Jesus confirmed the importance of the word of God when He was tempted by Satan to turn a stone into bread to sate His hunger:

> *And Jesus answered him, saying, it is written, that man shall not live by bread alone, but by every word of God.* (Luke 4:4 KJV)

When praying for His disciples at the last supper before His arrest, again Jesus focused on the truth of the word of God when He prayed:

> *Sanctify them through thy truth: thy word is truth.* (John 17:17 KJV)

Jesus affirmed that the word of God is the truth.

God says that He gives His word to accomplish His purpose, and it will not return to Him without having completed what He gave it for.[391] *The Bible* confirms that God has given His word as a guide in life, and to save people from destruction.[392]

Believing God's word and acting in obedience to it brings a blessing, and acting in unbelief and disobedience brings a curse.[393]

---

[390] Psalms 105:8.
[391] Isaiah 55:11.
[392] Psalms 17:4.
[393] Proverbs 13:13-14.

The word of God, the truth, is a shield to everyone who trusts in it, and it is a reflection of the perfection of God.[394]

Everything that the Old Testament declares concerning the word of God, Jesus has confirmed. Jesus said that not even the tiniest piece of the word of God would fail to be accomplished:

> *For verily I say unto you, Till heaven and earth pass,*
> *one jot or one tittle shall in no wise pass from the law,*
> *till all be fulfilled.* (Matthew 5:18 KJV)

There is irrefutable, corroborated, testimony that Jesus is God. Jesus declares the same thing for His word that He declares for God's word, because they are one in the same:

> *Heaven and earth shall pass away: but my words shall*
> *not pass away.* (Luke 21:33 KJV)

Jesus echoed what God said, everyone who heeds his word is wise, and whoever ignores his word is a fool. The lives of people will be blessed or cursed according to whether they believe the words of Jesus, or ignore them:

> *And why call ye me, Lord, Lord, and do not the things*
> *which I say? Whosoever cometh to me, and heareth*
> *my sayings, and doeth them, I will shew you to whom*
> *he is like: he is like a man which built an house, and*
> *digged deep, and laid the foundation on a rock: and*
> *when the flood arose, the stream beat vehemently*
> *upon that house, and could not shake it: for it was*
> *founded upon a rock. But he that heareth, and doeth*
> *not, is like a man that without a foundation built an*
> *house upon the earth; against which the stream did*

---

[394] Psalms 18:30.

beat vehemently, and immediately it fell; and the ruin
of that house was great. (Luke 6:46-49 KJV)

Jesus promises that there will be storms in life, and if the lives of people are not founded on the word of God, they will be destroyed.

Jesus only spoke what God gave Him to speak.[395] The very words of God and Jesus are life itself. Every word of God and every word of Jesus is true and trustworthy.

6.2 God Created the Universe and All Life

Unbelievers deny the word of God and the story of the creation, and often say that science shows it is not true. Many use a belief in evolution to deny the existence of God. They say that science has proven evolution and therefore there is no God. Belief in God must have come about because primitive peoples were trying to understand the world they lived in. In actuality, science has neither proven evolution nor disproven the existence of God.

What science has shown is that the universe came about at a point in time, that the scientists call "The Big Bang," and they have no explanation for it. Matter, energy, time, and the laws of physics that govern their interactions came into being at the same time as the universe. None of the natural forces that exist could have been responsible for the creation of the universe, because before the universe existed, they didn't exist either.

Furthermore, science has no evidence of evolution actually occurring. There has never been a single documented case of one type of life evolving into another type of life. All of science has shown that the types are separate and distinct. [396] Any variability

---

[395] John 14:10, 17:8.
[396] *Evolution, Still A Theory in Crisis,* by Michael Denton. Copyright ã 2016 Discovery Institute.

within a type has been shown to be adaptation according to the range allowed for that type by its DNA, what might be called microevolution. There has never been a single case that scientists could point to showing one type of life evolving into another, or what would be called macroevolution.

Not only that, but not a single scientist has been able to show a concrete mechanism that would allow one type of life to evolve into another.[397] Every scientific paper that talks about the evolution of the cell, or the evolution of any feature of life always states that the mechanism of evolution is not yet understood. They always explain their ignorance of the mechanisms of evolution by saying that with more time, it will all be understood. But that's not science; it is faith in naturalism without evidence.

They postulate the use of mutations and natural selection to drive evolution, but science has shown in every case, that every mutation that an organism experiences due to its environment, i.e., toxins, radiation, etc. was detrimental to the organism and typically the organism died. Never has a mutation that could cause a change in type been proven to have been passed down to offspring of the organism.

The scientists dogmatically cling to evolution even when faced with the facts that contradict it. They reject God's witness to the creation, not because there is not evidence that God created the universe out of nothing, but because they refuse to submit to the truth of God and acknowledge His right to judge their lives.

The Bible tells us that the whole universe testifies to the existence of God,[398] to His infinite wisdom and understanding, and His invisible power.[399] Science is very good at understanding repeatable events that it can observe over and over. But the creation of the universe and life was a one-time, supernatural

---

[397] *Darwin's Black Box: The Biochemical Challenge to Evolution*, by Michael Behe. Copyright ã 1996, 2006 Free Press.

[398] Psalms 19:1-3.

[399] Romans 1:20.

event, contrary to the laws of physics. Science will never be able to explain it, because science is the observation of natural events. Without the eyewitness testimony of an observer at the creation of the universe, there would be nothing known about it. God created the universe out of nothing; there were no raw materials.[400] *The Bible* tells us that God created everything:

> *In the beginning God created the heaven and the earth.* (Genesis 1:1 KJV)

God is the only eyewitness to the creation. God tells us to lift up our eyes to the sky and understand who made everything:

> *"To whom then will you liken Me, or to whom shall I be equal?" says the Holy One. Lift up your eyes on high, and see who has created these things, who brings out their host by number; He calls them all by name, by the greatness of His might and the strength of His power; not one is missing.* (Isaiah 40:25-26 NKJV)

God reiterates over and over that it is He who has created everything:

> *Thus says God the Lord, who created the heavens and stretched them out, who spread forth the earth and that which comes from it, who gives breath to the people on it, and spirit to those who walk on it.* (Isaiah 42:5-7 NKJV)

God rebukes man for disbelieving His record of the creation, and He says the same thing to people today that He said to Job:

---

[400] Hebrews 11:3.

"Where were you when I laid the foundations of the earth? Tell Me, if you have understanding. Who determined its measurements? Surely you know! Or who stretched the line upon it? To what were its foundations fastened? Or who laid its cornerstone? (Job 38:4-6 NKJV)

The doctrine of Christ confirms that God created the heavens and the earth, and all life. When the Pharisees questioned Jesus about divorce, He confirmed that God created man and woman and ordained marriage between them:

And he answered and said unto them, have ye not read, that he which made them at the beginning made them male and female, and said, for this cause shall a man leave father and mother, and shall cleave to his wife: and they twain shall be one flesh? Wherefore they are no more twain, but one flesh. What therefore God hath joined together, let not man put asunder. (Matthew 19:4-6 KJV)

In the beginning God made them male and female. Later when Jesus was talking to the disciples about the coming tribulation of the last days, He again confirmed that God created everything:

For in those days shall be affliction, such as was not from the beginning of the creation which God created unto this time, neither shall be. (Mark 13:19 KJV)

The tribulation was going to be greater than anything that had ever happened since God created the world and mankind, and there would never be another time like it in the future.

It is known that Jesus was also an eyewitness to the creation of the universe, because of His statement that he had been with God from before the foundation of the world:

> And now, O Father, glorify thou me with thine own self with the glory which I had with thee before the world was. (John 17:5 KJV)

Jesus confirmed that God was the creator of heaven and earth and all life. He was an eyewitness of creation, and His resurrection proves that his testimony is reliable.

6.3 Man Has a Responsibility to His Creator

Jesus confirmed that God created us; therefore we have a responsibility to God as our creator. He fashioned us, He made us, and He owns us. Mankind hates the thought that he is responsible to someone else who judges him. We are not our own, but God's, by right of creation.[401] God has the right to command our obedience to His standard of righteousness.

Jesus was questioned by the lawyer asking Him what was the great commandment in the law:

> Master, which is the great commandment in the law? Jesus said unto him, thou shalt love the Lord thy God with all thy heart, and with all thy soul, and with all thy mind. This is the first and great commandment. And the second is like unto it, thou shalt love thy neighbour as thyself. On these two commandments hang all the law and the prophets. (Matthew 22:36-40)

The doctrine of Christ is that we are commanded to love God with every fiber of our being and love our neighbors as ourselves.

---

[401] Psalms 100:3.

Jesus confirmed that everyone is our neighbor.[402] We are to walk in love towards God and man. We have a responsibility to obey the Lord God, our creator. If we don't, we will be found guilty when we stand before Him at the last judgment.

Jesus said that we demonstrate our love to God when we are obedient to His commandments:

> *If ye love me, keep my commandments. ... As the Father hath loved me, so have I loved you: continue ye in my love. If ye keep my commandments, ye shall abide in my love; even as I have kept my Father's commandments, and abide in his love. (John 14:15, 15:9-10)*

Man has a responsibility to God whether he likes it or not. Ever since the creation of mankind, man in his rebellion has been trying to throw off his responsibility to the God who created him. But God won't allow it, and laughs at the foolishness of men who think they can live apart from their creator without giving an account to Him.[403]

God has judged man in the past for his departing from the righteousness of God. *The Bible* tells us that the world of Noah was exceedingly sinful; every thought of the heart of man was evil:

> *And God saw that the wickedness of man was great in the earth, and that every imagination of the thoughts of his heart was only evil continually. (Genesis 6:5 KJV)*

The evil in the heart of man led to the earth being full of violence. Mankind was totally corrupt:

---

[402] Luke 10:29-37.
[403] Psalms 2:1-6.

The earth also was corrupt before God, and the earth was filled with violence. And God looked upon the earth, and, behold, it was corrupt; for all flesh had corrupted his way upon the earth. (Genesis 6:11-12 KJV)

Moses reports in the book of Genesis that God's judgment against the sin of Noah's world was to destroy the earth and all life on it except for Noah, his family, and the animals saved in the ark:

And, behold, I, even I, do bring a flood of waters upon the earth, to destroy all flesh, wherein is the breath of life, from under heaven; and every thing that is in the earth shall die. But with thee will I establish my covenant; and thou shalt come into the ark, thou, and thy sons, and thy wife, and thy sons' wives with thee. And of every living thing of all flesh, two of every sort shalt thou bring into the ark, to keep them alive with thee; they shall be male and female. Of fowls after their kind, and of cattle after their kind, of every creeping thing of the earth after his kind, two of every sort shall come unto thee, to keep them alive. (Genesis 6:17-20 KJV)

Unbelievers laugh at the story of the ark and the flood, but Jesus Christ confirmed that God destroyed the people living at Noah's time with a worldwide cataclysmic flood. Jesus said that judgment is coming on this world for the same reasons that God brought judgment on the anti-diluvian world, because of sin, violence, wickedness and corruption. And it will be the same when judgment falls on the modern world, people won't know it's coming until it's too late:

> *But of that day and hour knoweth no man, no, not the angels of heaven, but my Father only. But as the days of Noe were, so shall also the coming of the Son of man be. For as in the days that were before the flood they were eating and drinking, marrying and giving in marriage, until the day that Noe entered into the ark, and knew not until the flood came, and took them all away; so shall also the coming of the Son of man be.* (Matthew 24:36-39 KJV)

We cannot escape our responsibility to our creator. The doctrine of Christ is that every man is going to be judged for his failure to live up to God's commands. Each man will receive the just measure of his actions.[404]

The time of our judgment is fixed, and known to God alone. We will stand before our creator and give an account of our lives. Jesus told us to be afraid of failing to meet the righteous requirements of the Lord God:

> *And I say unto you my friends, be not afraid of them that kill the body, and after that have no more that they can do. But I will forewarn you whom ye shall fear: fear him, which after he hath killed hath power to cast into hell; yea, I say unto you, fear him.* (Luke 12:4-5 KJV)

There is a life after death. The God who created us is going to judge us, and there is a punishment for those who fail to meet God's standard of righteousness.

---

[404] Luke 12:40, 47-48.

6.4 God's Standard of Righteousness

Christ promised that those who fell short of God's standard of righteous would be condemned. What is God's standard of righteousness? How can we meet it? Earlier in the chapter on **"How Can We Know the Truth?,"** it was asked if God would accept us if we're good, and how good do we need to be? Jesus answered that question in the Sermon on the Mount:

> *Be ye therefore perfect, even as your Father which is in heaven is perfect.* (Matthew 5:48 KJV)

And, just so we wouldn't misunderstand what He meant by perfection, He said that one must be perfect in the thoughts of his heart, in the words of his mouth, and in the actions that spring from them.

Every word that someone has ever spoken will be remembered and brought into judgment:

> *But I say unto you, that every idle word that men shall speak, they shall give account thereof in the day of judgment. For by thy words thou shalt be justified, and by thy words thou shalt be condemned.* (Matthew 12:36-37 KJV)

God said, *"Thou shalt not kill,"*[405] and Jesus said that unjust hatred is murder.[406]

God said, *"Thou shalt not commit adultery,"*[407] and Jesus said that if someone even looks on someone other than their spouse with sexual desire, they've committed adultery.[408] Furthermore,

---

[405] Exodus 20:13 KJV.

[406] Matthew 5:22.

[407] Exodus 20:14 KJV.

[408] Matthew 5:28.

Jesus said that anyone who divorced his wife and married another was guilty of adultery, and anyone who married his divorced wife was committing adultery.[409]

Jesus said that people are to forswear vengeance. They are not to take vengeance on someone who has wronged them.[410] They are to love not only their friends, but also their enemies. They are to bless those people who curse them.[411]

God commanded that no one is to lie or to bear false witness, *"Thou shalt not bear false witness against thy neighbour."*[412] Jesus said Satan is the author of lies.[413] Bearing false witness does not only mean when someone testifies falsely against someone else. It means anytime someone affirms a lie to be the truth. When someone lies they are exhibiting the character of Satan.

God commanded people not to covet: *"Thou shalt not covet."*[414] People are not to desire anything that someone else has that they don't. They are not to let the desire for money and things come between God and them. They are not to treasure or worship anything other than God. Jesus said that it is impossible to serve two masters. No one can serve God and money.[415]

Jesus said to *"Render therefore unto Caesar the things that are Caesars; and unto God the things that are God's."*[416] He said this in the context of the Pharisees asking if it was lawful to pay taxes (tribute) to Rome. Jesus confirmed that God expects people to submit to the authority of governments and pay taxes.

To everyone who says, "I'm a good person," how do you

---

[409] Matthew 5:32.
[410] Matthew 5:38-39.
[411] Matthew 5:44.
[412] Exodus 20:16 KJV.
[413] John 8:44.
[414] Exodus 20:17 KJV.
[415] Matthew 6:19-21,24.
[416] Matthew 22:21.

answer to the requirement for perfection that comes from the righteousness of God?

Have you ever disobeyed your parents? Have you ever lied? Have you ever stolen anything? Have you ever thought evil of someone else because they had something that you wanted? Have you allowed the desire for money and riches to be more important than everything else in your life? Have you ever cheated on your taxes?

Have you ever been so angry with someone that you wished their death or thought of killing them? Have you ever said of someone who wronged you, "I'm going to do to him exactly what he's done to me?"

Have you ever lusted after someone who was not yours to have? Have you ever had a sexual relationship with someone you weren't married to? Have you divorced your wife or your husband?

A young ruler came up to Jesus and said that he had kept all of the commandments of God since his youth. He was lying to himself, but even if he had done all that he said, he still hadn't lived up to God's perfection.[417] Jesus told him that if he wanted to be perfect, there was more he must do.

God requires perfection, but the heart of man is evil. Jesus said that it's what's inside of a man or woman that corrupts them:

> *And he said, that which cometh out of the man, that defileth the man. For from within, out of the heart of men, proceed evil thoughts, adulteries, fornications, murders, thefts, covetousness, wickedness, deceit, lasciviousness, an evil eye, blasphemy, pride, foolishness: all these evil things come from within, and defile the man.* (Mark 7:20-23 KJV)

All sin is rebellion. Rebellion starts as soon as one is old

---
[417] Matthew 19:17-22.

enough to say "No" to his parents. People are in rebellion to the characterization of themselves as sinners in the word of God. Anyone who truly examines himself knows that God's word is true. But they don't want to listen. Jesus says their ears are hard of hearing and they've closed their eyes.[418] Everyone has fallen far short of God's standard. Everyone is corrupted by what's in his heart. They choose to do the evil that God hates. Everyone has failed to live up to the perfection required by the righteousness of God.

People carry the seeds of their own destruction within them. David said that there is no one who does good, everyone is corrupt.[419] Solomon said there is not a just man on the earth who doesn't sin.[420] In the Old Testament God says that the penalty for any sin is death:

> *Behold, all souls are mine; as the soul of the father, so*
> *also the soul of the son is mine: the soul that sinneth,*
> *it shall die.* (Ezekiel 18:4 KJV)

Again we see God claiming ownership of the people He created, and exerting His right to judge them. If anyone has ever broken any part of God's law, they're guilty. It doesn't matter if they're trying to keep His commandments now (an impossible task). If they've broken any part of the law at any time in their lives, they are condemned.

No one can hide anything from God their creator. The author of Hebrews says that everyone stands naked before the God to whom they must give an account.[421] Jesus said that there is nothing that can be kept secret:

---

[418] Matthew 13:15.

[419] Psalms 14:1-3.

[420] Ecclesiastes 7:20.

[421] Hebrews 4:13.

For there is nothing covered, that shall not be revealed;
neither hid, that shall not be known. (Luke 12:2 KJV)

Every failure to live up to God's righteousness will be known. Every deviation from the commands of God will be remembered. God will judge every thought, every word, and every action.

Jesus said there is no one who is good. No one has measured up to God's standard of righteousness; it's impossible. It is a standard of infinite perfection, because it is a reflection of the infinite righteousness of God. Everyone has failed to live up to the perfection of the righteousness of God. Everyone is condemned to death for his or her sin.

6.5 Jesus is the Only Way to God

Throughout history, mankind has tried to find a way to approach God on man's terms. Every religion other than Christianity, says, "Do this and God will accept you." It is man making a way to approach God. It is man saying that he deserves acceptance from God because of his goodness, because of what he has done. Mankind thinks that he has earned God's acceptance, and God should be in debt to him. Yet, as has been shown, no one has measured up to the goodness of God.

God will never accept man on man's terms. God says that man's righteousness is no more than filthy rags:

> *But we are all as an unclean thing, and all our*
> *righteousnesses are as filthy rags; and we all do fade*
> *as a leaf; and our iniquities, like the wind, have taken*
> *us away.* (Isaiah 64:6 KJV)

6.5.1 Salvation in Christ Alone

God knew that mankind could never live up to His perfect standard of righteous, that it is impossible. How could God reconcile the requirement of His righteousness that sin must be punished with death, with His love for man whom He created and His desire to save his life? In the councils of God in eternity past, God the Father, God the Son, and God the Holy Spirit determined how to save mankind even before he had been created. Jesus is called, *"The lamb slain from the foundation of the world."*[422]

What mankind could never do, God did. He made a way for men and women to be cleansed of their sin so they could approach Him. The Son of God planned to become a sacrifice to pay for the sins of men and women. The punishment that God's righteousness required against sin would be meted out to Christ on the cross. Anyone who puts his trust in Jesus Christ as his savior would be forgiven, would be justified, and would no longer be under the wrath of God for sin.[423] Jesus is the Lamb of God, and He was going to sacrifice His life to redeem or ransom people from sin.[424]

Jesus told Nicodemus that whoever believed in Him would not perish, but would have everlasting life.[425] Jesus came to save people from the righteous wrath of God.[426] Anyone who refuses to believe in Christ is condemned already because they refuse to believe in the only Son of God:

> *He that believeth on him is not condemned: but he that believeth not is condemned already, because he hath not believed in the name of the only begotten Son of God. ... He that believeth on the Son hath*

---

[422] Revelation 13:8 KJV.
[423] Romans 5:9.
[424] Mark 10:45.
[425] John 3:15.
[426] John 3:16-17.

everlasting life: and he that believeth not the Son shall
not see life; but the wrath of God abideth on him.
(John 3:18,36 KJV)

The whole world is under condemnation for rebellion against God. Everyone has sinned, and the penalty for sin is death. Everyone is already condemned. It is impossible for people to live a life good enough for God to accept them; everyone has already failed. David prayed that God would not judge him, because he knew that he didn't measure up to the righteousness of God:

And enter not into judgment with thy servant: for
in thy sight shall no man living be justified. (Psalms
143:2 KJV)

The wrath of God is abiding on people. They can only escape the wrath of God that their sin deserves by trusting in Jesus to save them.

Some of the disciples told Jesus about some Galileans who had been executed by Pilate, who had then mingled their blood with their sacrifices. Jesus asked them if they thought those Galileans were worse sinners than others? He told them that those people who suffered that death were no different than anyone else. Jesus asked the disciples if the eighteen people who died when a tower in Siloam fell on them were worse than other people? Did their deaths come about because they were worse sinners than other men? Jesus said no, they were no worse than anyone else. Jesus told them that everyone would likewise perish unless they repent.[427]

At one point in his ministry, Jesus asked the disciples if they also wanted to leave Him:

---

[427] Luke 13:1-5.

> *Then said Jesus unto the twelve, will ye also go away?*
> *Then Simon Peter answered him, Lord, to whom shall*
> *we go? Thou hast the words of eternal life. And we*
> *believe and are sure that thou art that Christ, the Son*
> *of the living God.* (John 6:68 KJV)

Peter said there was no one else they could turn to; Jesus Christ had the words of life. Later when speaking to the Jews, Jesus told them that if they didn't believe that He is the Christ, sent by God to save them, they would die in their sins:

> *I said therefore unto you, that ye shall die in your sins:*
> *for if ye believe not that I am he, ye shall die in your*
> *sins.* (John 8:24 KJV)

All without Christ will be judged and die because of their sin. The only escape from the judgment of God is the forgiveness found in Christ.

Jesus returned to Bethany four days after the death of Lazarus. Lazarus' sister, Martha, was asking Jesus why He had not returned in time to heal her brother?[428] Jesus told Martha:

> *"... I am the resurrection, and the life: he that*
> *believeth in me, though he were dead, yet shall he*
> *live: and whosoever liveth and believeth in me shall*
> *never die ..."* (John 11:25-26 KJV)

Jesus told Martha that only in Him could people live forever. Jesus stated that He is the one who resurrects the dead, and keeps the living from dying. Jesus is the only one who has life in Himself and can give life to others. [429] Every other religion contradicts the

---

[428] John 11:21.
[429] John 5:25-27, John 8:51, John 17:2.

truth of Christ and is in error because Jesus said that He is the only way to God:

> *Jesus saith unto him, I am the way, the truth, and the life: no man cometh unto the Father, but by me.* (John 14:6 KJV).

There is no one else that we can turn to. Jesus has the words of eternal life, and only Jesus has been given to us for salvation:

> *Neither is there salvation in any other: for there is none other name under heaven given among men, whereby we must be saved.* (Acts 4:12 KJV)

6.5.2 Salvation Through Christ Brings Division

The exclusivity of salvation through Christ alone brings division. Jesus told people that He would bring division on the earth:

> *Suppose ye that I am come to give peace on earth? I tell you, nay; but rather division: for from henceforth there shall be five in one house divided, three against two, and two against three. The father shall be divided against the son, and the son against the father; the mother against the daughter, and the daughter against the mother; the mother in law against her daughter in law, and the daughter in law against her mother in law.* (Luke 12:51-53 KJV)

The belief in the truth of God and Christ, or its rejection, is so important that it will divide families. Anyone who puts self or family above Christ and God is not worthy of Christ,[430] and

---

[430] Matthew 10:37-38.

cannot be His disciple.[431] People either acknowledge that God and Christ are supreme in their lives, or they let something or someone else take their place.

In multiple ways Jesus told people that there are only two groups in the world, those who are with God and Christ, and those who are against God and Christ. There are no other groups or classes of people.

The disciples asked Jesus if there were only a few people who would be saved.[432] Jesus told the disciples that there is a small group of people who are entering into heaven on the narrow path through the narrow gate. Jesus is that narrow gate.[433] But there are many people who are on the broad highway heading through the wide gate to destruction.[434] They think they are walking on a good road, but it leads to death.[435]

At another time Jesus told the disciples that whoever wanted to come after Him had to deny themselves, take up their cross, and follow Him.[436] The narrow path through the narrow gate is a denial of self, and a following of Jesus Christ, no matter what the consequences in this life. Those walking on the broad highway are those who ignore the word of Christ so they can go their own way, so that they can indulge themselves in their own desires.

Jesus told people that, whoever hates Him, hates God.[437] Someone can't love God and hate Christ. God and Christ are one.[438] All people who believe in Christ and give their lives to

---

[431] Luke 14:26.
[432] Luke 13:23-27.
[433] John 10:7.
[434] Matthew 7:13.
[435] Proverbs 16:25.
[436] Mark 8:34.
[437] John 15:23.
[438] John 17:21.

Him are one with Him and God.[439] Anyone who rejects Christ is rejecting God as well.[440]

Jesus stated that whoever does not honor Him, does not honor God the Father either.[441] Jesus is worthy of the honor that belongs only to God. People either honor Christ, or they dishonor both Him and God.

Jesus stated that only His word would be allowed to bear permanent fruit in the earth. His doctrine is the doctrine of God and Jesus speaks the truth of God. Every plant that hasn't been planted by God will be uprooted.[442] Anyone following another doctrine will not remain. Jesus called them, *"Blind leaders of the blind,"* and promised that they both would fall.[443]

No one can approach God except through the way that God made, the sacrifice of Jesus for sin. Christians are not being religious bigots when they report that there is salvation in no one other than Jesus Christ. They are simply reporting what Jesus Himself has said. It has been confirmed that Jesus has spoken the truth about salvation, because every witness has corroborated his testimony. No one should let the stark truth of what Jesus has said about sin and salvation lead them to deny the salvation that is found in Christ alone.

6.6 You Must Be Born Again

Jesus confirmed that Satan has a kingdom and he is the ruler of this world.[444] How does God take someone from the kingdom of Satan and bring him or her into the kingdom of God? How does

---

[439] John 17:22-23.
[440] 1 John 2:23.
[441] John 5:21-23.
[442] Matthew 15:13.
[443] Matthew 15:14.
[444] Matthew 12:25-26; John 12:31, 14:30, 16:11.

someone take advantage of the forgiveness that is found in Christ and receive the gift of eternal life?

Paul says that nothing that someone does in the flesh is pleasing to God; instead their carnal nature is at war with God:

> For they that are after the flesh do mind the things of the flesh; but they that are after the Spirit the things of the Spirit. For to be carnally minded is death; but to be spiritually minded is life and peace. Because the carnal mind is enmity against God: for it is not subject to the law of God, neither indeed can be. So then they that are in the flesh cannot please God. (Romans 8:5-8 KJV)

Jesus didn't come to the earth to give mankind a new moral code to live by, a new set of rules whereby someone can be accepted by God. Nothing that the natural man can do is pleasing to God. The recorded history of man on earth shows that he is totally corrupt and unclean.[445]

God, when speaking of Israel, says that He did everything possible for His people to bring forth good fruit, but all they produced was wild fruit. It wasn't because the Israelites were worse sinners than other men; it is because men have corrupted their way and cannot produce good fruit.[446]

Jesus said that every tree that doesn't bear good fruit would be chopped down:

> And now also the axe is laid unto the root of the trees: therefore every tree which bringeth not forth good fruit is hewn down, and cast into the fire. (Matthew 3:10 KJV)

---

[445] Isaiah 64:6.
[446] Isaiah 5:1-7.

The desire of God's heart is that all men would learn the truth of God and Christ and be saved:

> *Who will have all men to be saved, and to come unto*
> *the knowledge of the truth. For there is one God, and*
> *one mediator between God and men, the man Christ*
> *Jesus; who gave himself a ransom for all, to be testified*
> *in due time.* (1 Timothy 2:4-5 KJV)

Jesus stated that one must be born again in order to enter into the kingdom of Heaven:

> *Jesus answered and said unto him, Verily, verily, I*
> *say unto thee, except a man be born again, he cannot*
> *see the kingdom of God. ... Jesus answered, Verily,*
> *verily, I say unto thee, except a man be born of water*
> *and of the Spirit, he cannot enter into the kingdom of*
> *God.* (John 3:3,5 KJV)

Jesus said that which is born of the flesh is flesh and that which is born of the Spirit is spirit.[447] It is not something that can be seen or felt, it is a spiritual birth.[448]

John tells us that it is not a birth that comes from the will of man, but from the will of God. It is a spiritual birth given to anyone who receives Jesus as the Son of God:

> *But as many as received him, to them gave he power*
> *to become the sons of God, even to them that believe*
> *on his name: which were born, not of blood, nor of*
> *the will of the flesh, nor of the will of man, but of*
> *God.* (John 1:12-13 KJV)

---

[447] John 3:6.
[448] John 3:8.

The new birth in the Spirit involves two aspects, repentance and faith or belief in Christ:

> *Now after that John was put in prison, Jesus came into Galilee, preaching the gospel of the kingdom of God, and saying, the time is fulfilled, and the kingdom of God is at hand: repent ye, and believe the gospel.* (Mark 1:15 KJV)

Repentance is when one acknowledges that God is right and he is wrong. Repentance means to turn from going one's own way, from following one's own wisdom, and turn towards God and His way. Jesus said that He came to call sinners to repentance:

> *But go ye and learn what that meaneth, I will have mercy, and not sacrifice: for I am not come to call the righteous, but sinners to repentance.* (Matthew 9:13 KJV)

Jesus promised that whoever won't repent, will perish.[449]

Jesus said that Nineveh repented at the preaching of the prophet Jonah. Jesus is greater than the prophet Jonah and everyone needs to repent at his preaching. Jonah was a sign to the Ninevites because of his being cast into the belly of the fish [KJV: whale] for three days.[450] The resurrection of Jesus is the sign beckoning to everyone to repent and believe the Gospel.[451]

Paul says that godly sorrow works repentance and leads people to salvation.[452] And it is the patience and goodness of God that leads people to repentance:

---

[449] Luke 13:1-5.

[450] Luke 11:30.

[451] Matthew 12:39-41.

[452] 2 Corinthians 7:10.

> *Or do you despise the riches of His goodness,*
> *forbearance, and longsuffering, not knowing that the*
> *goodness of God leads you to repentance?* (Romans
> 2:4 NKJV)

There is no forgiveness or salvation for someone if he refuses to repent of going his own way and ignoring God. It doesn't matter if he's sorry about his sin. Judas was remorseful over his betrayal of Christ, but was unwilling to repent of going his own way, and believe in Christ for forgiveness.[453]

It doesn't matter if one believes that Jesus is the Son of God. Each person must renounce his sin and turn to God for forgiveness and pray for Him to lead him in righteousness. The author of the book of Hebrews says that when someone repents he is really repenting from dead works, from the works of the natural man that only lead to death.[454] In the book of Revelation Jesus says that He chastens everyone He loves so that they will repent.[455]

During the time of the tribulation, the people will be condemned because they refuse to repent of their evil and turn to God for forgiveness.[456] No matter what judgment God brings in the future on the men who reject Christ, they refuse to repent of their evil deeds.

Part of repentance is coming to see the evil of departing from God to follow a different path, and to understand that it is rebellion. Repentance means to acknowledge the truth of *The Bible* when it says that men and women are sinners. They are not sinners because they sin. They sin because they are sinners. The conviction of the Holy Spirit leads people to sorrow over their rebellion and helps them to understand the difference between

---

[453] Matthew 27:3-5.

[454] Hebrews 6:1; Provervs 14:12.

[455] Revelation 3:19.

[456] Revelation 9:20-21, 16:9-11.

whom they thought they were and who they really are in God's eyes. Everyone has fallen far short of the glory of God.[457]

But someone is not born again just because they repent. They're born again when their repentance leads them to believe the word of God and believe in Him whom He sent, Jesus Christ. They must believe that Jesus is the Christ, the Lamb of God, who paid for their sins on the cross. They must believe that the death of Christ is the atoning sacrifice for their sin. They must believe that the resurrected Jesus is their Lord and submit their lives to him. They must believe in the testimony of Christ, and renounce all hope of salvation in anyone else:

> *That if thou shalt confess with thy mouth the Lord Jesus, and shalt believe in thine heart that God hath raised him from the dead, thou shalt be saved. For with the heart man believeth unto righteousness; and with the mouth confession is made unto salvation. ... For whosoever shall call upon the name of the Lord shall be saved.* (Romans 10:9-10,13 KJV)

When both of these are true, repentance and belief in Christ as Lord and Savior, they are born again by the Holy Spirit of God. They are adopted into the family of God as His sons and daughters. The Holy Spirit is now living in them, and they call God their Father:

> *For ye have not received the spirit of bondage again to fear; but ye have received the Spirit of adoption, whereby we cry, Abba, Father. The Spirit itself beareth witness with our spirit, that we are the children of God.* (Romans 8:15-16 KJV)

---

[457] Romans 3:23.

The redemption of Christ has made possible their adoption as the sons and daughters of a Holy God:

> *But when the fulness of the time was come, God sent forth his Son, made of a woman, made under the law, to redeem them that were under the law, that we might receive the adoption of sons. And because ye are sons, God hath sent forth the Spirit of his Son into your hearts, crying, Abba, Father. Wherefore thou art no more a servant, but a son; and if a son, then an heir of God through Christ.* (Galatians 4:4-7 KJV)

Peter says that because of the resurrection of Christ, Christians have been born again to a living hope:

> *Blessed be the God and Father of our Lord Jesus Christ, who according to His abundant mercy has begotten us again to a living hope through the resurrection of Jesus Christ from the dead, to an inheritance incorruptible and undefiled and that does not fade away, reserved in heaven for you, who are kept by the power of God through faith for salvation ready to be revealed in the last time.* (1 Peter 1:3-5 NKJV)

Christians have been born again to a living hope in Christ and in God's word. They are children of God and joint heirs with Christ.[458] They are no longer children of the world.[459] Christians walk in faith towards God and Christ.[460]

The new birth means to be born again to the everlasting life

---

[458] Romans 8:17.
[459] John 17:14.
[460] 2 Corinthians 5:7.

of God. Not just an unending life, but a new life in Christ, the life of the uncreated, eternal God, a life whereby they are made partakers of the divine nature.[461] It is a life that is different than what the natural man experiences now. Jesus said that he came to give people eternal life, and it would be an abundant life. It is the life of Christ himself:

> *The thief cometh not, but for to steal, and to kill, and to destroy: I am come that they might have life, and that they might have it more abundantly.* (John 10:10 KJV)

It is God who has justified the believer.[462] God takes his sin and applies it to Christ's death on the cross, and applies Christ's righteousness to him. He stands before God in the righteousness of Christ:

> *For he hath made him to be sin for us, who knew no sin; that we might be made the righteousness of God in him.* (2 Corinthians 5:21 KJV)

A life in the flesh on this earth, which ends in death, is traded for an abundant eternal life in the Spirit with Christ and God forever.

The sins of each Christian, past, present, and future were nailed to the cross of Christ.[463] He is no longer fearful of judgment, but comes into the presence of God with joy knowing what God has done for him in Christ. In Christ there is assurance of forgiveness.[464] In Christ there is assurance of righteousness.[465]

---

[461] 2 Peter 1:2-4.

[462] Romans 8:33.

[463] Colossians 2:13-14.

[464] Ephesians 1:7.

[465] Galatians 5:5.

Christians have the peace of Christ given to them to keep them from being moved by the trials and tribulations that come in this life.[466] God is for every Christian.[467]

The new birth by the Holy Spirit of God gives every Christian a desire to know God and His word, and to walk in holiness before Him. He has a new love for God that He imparts to him. The sons and daughters of God want to draw close to Him. They want to worship Him in the manner He desires, in spirit and in truth.[468] They don't want anything in their lives that displeases Him. They want to cleanse themselves of everything that defiles them and grieves their Lord:

> *Having therefore these promises, dearly beloved, let us cleanse ourselves from all filthiness of the flesh and spirit, perfecting holiness in the fear of God. (2 Corinthians 7:1 KJV)*

Not only are Christians forgiven and saved, but also they are created in Christ for good works. God has something special for each of them to do that will bless their lives and the lives of people around them. They are no longer living only for themselves, but are called to a higher purpose in Christ.[469]

Peter asked Christ what the disciples would receive for having forsaken all to follow Christ? Christ promised them a new family and new possessions, but with persecutions.[470] But Christians don't follow Christ because of any material blessings here, and they don't let the persecutions that come from those who don't know Christ sway them from faithfulness to God. They follow Christ because

---

[466] John 14:27.
[467] Romans 8:31-32.
[468] John 4:23-24.
[469] Romans 8:28-30; Ephesians 2:10.
[470] Mark 10:28-31.

He is the only one who has the words of life. His sacrifice has given them eternal life together with a Holy God.

Every Christian is a brother or sister to every other Christian in the family of God. They have been redeemed from every tribe, and nation, and peoples, and tongues.[471] The divisions that separated them no longer stand between them. Even though the world without Christ will hate Christians if they're faithful to Him, their brothers and sisters in Christ will love them and honor them for their obedience.[472] They will give joy to each other because of their faith in God and His word.[473]

The disciples returned from their first missionary trip and were excited because even the demons had to flee before their authority in Christ. Jesus told them not to be excited about having power over demons, but to be excited because their names were written in heaven, in the *Lamb's Book of Life*.[474] Christians joy in the salvation of the Lord because their names are written in heaven and they won't be condemned in the judgment.[475]

Jesus tells people to come to Him and He will give them rest, rest from the things of the world, from the lies, injustice, hatred, doubt, and uncertainty for the future:

> Come unto me, all ye that labour and are heavy laden, and I will give you rest. Take my yoke upon you, and learn of me; for I am meek and lowly in heart: and ye shall find rest unto your souls. For my yoke is easy, and my burden is light. (Matthew 11:28-30 KJV)

---

[471] Revelation 5:9.
[472] Psalms 15:4.
[473] Psalms 119:74.
[474] Luke 10:17-20.
[475] Revelation 20:11-15.

Jesus is the only one who can remove the burden of sin and its righteous punishment coming in the future. Christians rest in the love of God and Christ for them and in the work of Christ on the cross. No one can take the everlasting life of Christ away from them.[476] They no longer have to be afraid of anything. Paul says that their lives are hidden with Christ in God. When they die to themselves and give their lives to God, He hides their lives in the life of Christ.[477] Ever after they have the Holy Spirit living in them.[478] God will never forsake them.[479] They have fellowship and joy in the presence of God.[480]

God's purpose in salvation is to conform all Christians to the image of Christ, to restore the image of God to them that they lost when they rebelled against God and went their own way.[481] They come to know the love of God, demonstrated when Jesus died for them, and displayed thereafter in their lives by the God who lives in them, a love that can never be taken from them.[482] The Holy Spirit pours out the love of God in their lives, and the perfect love of God casts out all fear.[483]

Not only are they forgiven and saved, but also they come into a personal relationship with the God who created them, never to be alone again. God is with them, and He knows them better than they know themselves. He is guiding them, demonstrating His love for them over and over. God works in them to perfect them, and one day they will stand before Him perfect and complete.[484]

In the world to come, God promises that He is going to create

---

[476] John 10:27-30, 11:25-27.

[477] Colossians 3:3.

[478] John 14:15-18.

[479] Hebrews 13:5.

[480] Psalms 16:11.

[481] Romans 8:29-30; 2 Corinthians 3:18.

[482] Romans 8:5.

[483] Romans 5:5; 2 Timothy 1:7; 1 John 4:18-19.

[484] Philippians 1:6; Jude 1:24-25.

a new heavens and a new earth where there will be no sin.[485] Accepting Christ means that in the future Christians get to live forever in a perfect world with no more pain, no more sorrow, and no more death.[486] God promises them that they will always be walking in the light of the countenance of Christ and God.[487] Everyone who has been saved by Christ will be their friends and neighbors, exercising graciousness, love, and affection towards each other. The sons and daughters of God will live in a perfect physical world with no decay; a world as perfect as only an all-knowing and all-powerful God can make it. Their resurrected bodies will be like that of Christ. They will have the same physical bodies as Christ Himself has chosen to live in for all of eternity.[488]

And it is going to take all of eternity for each Christian to understand the gift of eternal life that God has given him, the forgiveness found in Christ, the love of God, and His graciousness towards him. Christians will be in heaven, knowing they don't deserve what God has given them, but they get to receive it and enjoy it, and share it with Christ and with each other.

> But God, who is rich in mercy, because of His great love with which He loved us, even when we were dead in trespasses, made us alive together with Christ (by grace you have been saved), and raised us up together, and made us sit together in the heavenly places in Christ Jesus, that in the ages to come He might show the exceeding riches of His grace in His kindness toward us in Christ Jesus. For by grace you have been saved through faith, and that not of yourselves; it is the gift of God, not of works, lest anyone should boast. (Ephesians 2:4-9 NKJV)

---

[485] 2 Peter 3:10-13; Revelation 21:1

[486] Revelation 21:4.

[487] Revelations 21:23.

[488] Luke 24:39; 1 John 3:2.

David asked how he could repay the Lord for his salvation? Every son and daughter of God asks the same thing, what can they do to repay the Lord:

> *What shall I render unto the Lord for all his benefits toward me? I will take the cup of salvation, and call upon the name of the Lord.* (Psalms 116:12-13 KJV)

Jesus said that the water He gives them would be a well of water springing up into eternal life:

> *But whosoever drinketh of the water that I shall give him shall never thirst; but the water that I shall give him shall be in him a well of water springing up into everlasting life.* (John 4:14 KJV)

The water of life is the Holy Spirit of God, and Jesus promised all believers that the river of the water of life would flow from within them to water everything around them:

> *In the last day, that great day of the feast, Jesus stood and cried, saying, If any man thirst, let him come unto me, and drink. He that believeth on me, as the scripture hath said, out of his belly shall flow rivers of living water. (But this spake he of the Spirit, which they that believe on him should receive: for the Holy Ghost was not yet given; because that Jesus was not yet glorified.)* (John 7:37-39 KJV)

In the book of Revelation, Jesus Christ testifies that there is a river of the water of life flowing from the throne of God and Christ:

> And he shewed me a pure river of water of life, clear
> as crystal, proceeding out of the throne of God and of
> the Lamb. In the midst of the street of it, and on either
> side of the river, was there the tree of life, which bare
> twelve manner of fruits, and yielded her fruit every
> month: and the leaves of the tree were for the healing
> of the nations. (Revelation 22:1-2 KJV)

God, Christ, and the Holy Spirit are calling to people to forsake their ownselves and the world and come to the fountain of the water of life. The bride of Christ, the saints, are calling to everyone to come to the fountain of the water of life:

> I Jesus have sent mine angel to testify unto you these
> things in the churches. I am the root and the offspring
> of David, and the bright and morning star. And the
> Spirit and the bride say, come. And let him that
> heareth say, come. And let him that is athirst come.
> And whosoever will, let him take the water of life
> freely. (Revelation 22:16-17 KJV)

Jesus Christ is the source of life. Let everyone who will, come and drink of Christ, the fountain of the water of life.

6.7 Deny Yourself, Take Up Your Cross, and Follow Christ

Once someone has been born again, Christ calls on him to deny himself, take up his cross, and follow Him:

> Then said Jesus unto his disciples, if any man will
> come after me, let him deny himself, and take up his
> cross, and follow me. For whosoever will save his life
> shall lose it: and whosoever will lose his life for my
> sake shall find it. For what is a man profited, if he

shall gain the whole world, and lose his own soul?
Or what shall a man give in exchange for his soul?
(Matthew 16:24-26 KJV)

Believers submit to the lordship and authority of Christ. Paul says that because of what Christ has done for each Christian, it is his reasonable service to sacrifice his life for Christ.[489] He must deny himself and sacrifice his will to the will of God.

When God promised the Messiah that he would be a priest forever after the order of Melchizedek, He also promised Him that His people would be willing [NKJV:volunteers] in submission to Him:

Thy people shall be willing in the day of thy power,
in the beauties of holiness from the womb of the
morning: thou hast the dew of thy youth. (Psalms
110:3 KJV)

Christians have the life of Christ living in them and they willingly submit themselves to Christ in everything He calls on them to do in life.

The wisdom of the world is always calling people to exalt themselves and follow the dreams of their hearts. Jeremiah says that whoever listens to his own heart, lies to himself. The heart of man is wicked:

The heart is deceitful above all things, and desperately
wicked: who can know it? (Jeremiah 17:9 KJV)

Denying oneself means to obey the word of God always, especially when it contradicts what a person wants or thinks. Paul says that the old man of sin, the natural man, the man of the

---

[489] Romans 12:1.

flesh, has been crucified with Christ. Those who are born again are dead to sin and alive to Jesus Christ.[490] Denying oneself means to kneel before the Lord Christ and acknowledge that one has been set free from sin and has become a slave of righteousness because of the salvation Christ wrought.[491] Denying oneself means fighting against the old man, fighting against the lust of the flesh, the lust of the eyes, and the pride of life.[492] Christians humble themselves before Christ and other people. Speaking of Christ, John the Baptist said, *"He must increase, but I must decrease."*[493] Self-denial is a life-long spiritual battle of humbling oneself and exalting Christ.

Those born again in Christ battle against the thoughts and ideas of the world, which would deny Christ or remove Him from His place of pre-eminence:

> *For though we walk in the flesh, we do not war after the flesh: (for the weapons of our warfare are not carnal, but mighty through God to the pulling down of strong holds;) casting down imaginations, and every high thing that exalteth itself against the knowledge of God, and bringing into captivity every thought to the obedience of Christ;* (2 Corinthians 10:3-5 KJV)

Yet they are not alone in this battle. Jesus has given them His Holy Spirit to correct, to uphold, and to comfort them.[494] No matter how many times a believer fails, the Holy Spirit always brings him back to Christ for forgiveness and help. God has given every Christian the Holy Spirit to sanctify him, to separate him from this world, and to unite him with God and Christ.

---

490 Romans 6:6-8.
491 Romans 6:18.
492 1 John 2:16.
493 John 3:30 KJV.
494 John 14:15-18.

We have to die in Christ. In Psalms it tells us that the death of His saints is precious to God:

> *Precious in the sight of the Lord is the death of his saints.* (Psalms 116:15 KJV)

It's not just when a saint of God dies at the end of his life and goes to heaven to live forever with God, that God thinks his death is precious. Everyday dying to oneself and living to Christ is precious to God because it exalts His Son.

Every Christian takes up his cross by acknowledging that he is now dead to this world, with all of its lusts and desires that would draw him away from Christ. The cross is a reminder of what Christ has done for each believer, and a reminder that he suffers with Him in this world, awaiting His return and the establishment of His kingdom of righteousness:

> *The Spirit itself beareth witness with our spirit, that we are the children of God: and if children, then heirs; heirs of God, and joint-heirs with Christ; if so be that we suffer with him, that we may be also glorified together. For I reckon that the sufferings of this present time are not worthy to be compared with the glory which shall be revealed in us.* (Romans 8:16-18 KJV)

The cross is an acknowledgement that the believer is dead to sin and this world. It confirms the total denial of oneself so that his life might be hid with Christ in God.[495]

---

[495] Colossians 3:1-5.

> *So likewise, whosoever he be of you that forsaketh*
> *not all that he hath, he cannot be my disciple.* (Luke
> 14:33 KJV)

Christ said that those who lose their lives for His sake would find them.[496]

Throughout his ministry, Jesus told people to follow Him.[497] He called Matthew from his work as a tax collector and said, *"Follow me."*[498] Jesus told people that whoever didn't take up their cross and follow Him was not worthy of him:

> *He that loveth father or mother more than me is not*
> *worthy of me: and he that loveth son or daughter*
> *more than me is not worthy of me. And he that taketh*
> *not his cross, and followeth after me, is not worthy of*
> *me.* (Matthew 10:37-38 KJV)

Denying oneself, taking up one's cross, and following Christ, is a rejection of the world, its false promises, its hidden sorrow, and its death and future end, to gain what is eternal, right, and good. The sons and daughters of God have been made joint heirs with Christ of all of God's creation.[499] Jesus is commanding all of God's children to deny themselves and follow him because it is the only way to a better future. There is nothing in this world that is worth losing one's soul over, not one's relationships with people, not one's position, not one's possessions, and not one's dreams. Nothing compares to what one has in Christ, and His way is the only way.

Jesus promised that everyone who is His disciple would follow him. His disciples are the sheep of his pasture. They know his voice and they follow his call:

---

[496] Matthew 10:39.

[497] Matthew 8:19-22, 19:21.

[498] Matthew 9:9.

[499] Romans 8:16-17.

My sheep hear my voice, and I know them, and they follow me: and I give unto them eternal life; and they shall never perish, neither shall any man pluck them out of my hand. My Father, which gave them me, is greater than all; and no man is able to pluck them out of my Father's hand. I and my Father are one. (John 10:27-30 KJV)

Jesus said that he always did those things that pleased the Lord.[500] Jesus said that he glorified God in his life.[501] As the sons and daughters of God, as the disciples of Christ, our role in life is to glorify God the Father and Jesus Christ His Son. We are to live in a manner that leads other people to salvation, that holds up Christ for all to see. We are to live in a way that shows the love and beauty of Christ. Whatever he calls on us to do, we must do it with joy knowing that God has good plans for us.[502]

Christ told us that we could do nothing on our own. Only by following Christ, abiding in him, and letting his life abide in us can we accomplish anything eternal:

"I am the true vine, and My Father is the vinedresser. Every branch in Me that does not bear fruit He takes away; and every branch that bears fruit He prunes, that it may bear more fruit. You are already clean because of the word which I have spoken to you. Abide in Me, and I in you. As the branch cannot bear fruit of itself, unless it abides in the vine, neither can you, unless you abide in Me. (John 15:1-4 NKJV)

---

[500] John 8:29.
[501] John 17:4.
[502] Jeremiah 29:11-13.

> *"I am the vine, you are the branches. He who abides
> in Me, and I in him, bears much fruit; for without Me
> you can do nothing. If anyone does not abide in Me,
> he is cast out as a branch and is withered; and they
> gather them and throw them into the fire, and they
> are burned. If you abide in Me, and My words abide
> in you, you will ask what you desire, and it shall be
> done for you. By this My Father is glorified, that you
> bear much fruit; so you will be My disciples.* (John
> 15:5-8 NKJV)

To abide in Christ means to allow his word to dwell in one
richly. Abiding in Christ means to allow the Holy Spirit to bear
fruit in one's life. Abiding in Christ means to walk in the Holy
Spirit. The fruit of the Holy Spirit abiding in one's life brings glory
to God and Christ:

> *But the fruit of the Spirit is love, joy, peace,
> longsuffering, gentleness, goodness, faith, meekness,
> temperance: against such there is no law. And they
> that are Christ's have crucified the flesh with the
> affections and lusts. If we live in the Spirit, let us also
> walk in the Spirit.* (Galatians 5:22-25 KJV)

If someone doesn't have the life of Christ and the Holy Spirit
abiding in them, then they are dead, and dead branches produce
no fruit.

Following Christ means to obey his command for the disciples
to love one another. Christ said that every one is to love others as
Christ loved them, giving His life for them. When believers walk
in obedience to the word of God and Christ, they walk in their
love:

*As the Father hath loved me, so have I loved you:
continue ye in my love. If ye keep my commandments,
ye shall abide in my love; even as I have kept my
Father's commandments, and abide in his love. These
things have I spoken unto you, that my joy might
remain in you, and that your joy might be full. This
is my commandment, that ye love one another, as I
have loved you.* (John 15:9-12 KJV)

*Greater love hath no man than this, that a man lay
down his life for his friends. Ye are my friends, if ye
do whatsoever I command you. Henceforth I call you
not servants; for the servant knoweth not what his
lord doeth: but I have called you friends; for all things
that I have heard of my Father I have made known
unto you. Ye have not chosen me, but I have chosen
you, and ordained you, that ye should go and bring
forth fruit, and that your fruit should remain: that
whatsoever ye shall ask of the Father in my name, he
may give it you. These things I command you, that
ye love one another.* (John 15:13-17 KJV)

Whoever follows Christ, Jesus calls him His friend, and
promises him that his life will bear permanent fruit to the glory
of God.

The command of Christ to follow Him and obey His commands
means that no disciple should envy what Christ has called other
disciples to do. It doesn't matter what responsibilities the Lord
gives to other disciples. Each disciple has a responsibility to follow
whatever Christ tells them to do:

*Then Peter, turning around, saw the disciple whom
Jesus loved following, who also had leaned on His
breast at the supper, and said, "Lord, who is the one*

> *who betrays You?" Peter, seeing him, said to Jesus,*
> *"But Lord, what about this man?" Jesus said to him,*
> *"If I will that he remain till I come, what is that to*
> *you? You follow Me."* (John 21:20-22 NKJV)

Jesus Christ says the same thing to everyone of His disciples, *"You follow me."*

6.8 Jesus Will Return to Judge the World

Jesus promised that there is a judgment coming, a separation between the wicked and the righteous. He prophesied that he is going to return to judge the world:

> *When the Son of man shall come in his glory, and all*
> *the holy angels with him, then shall he sit upon the*
> *throne of his glory: and before him shall be gathered all*
> *nations: and he shall separate them one from another,*
> *as a shepherd divideth his sheep from the goats: and*
> *he shall set the sheep on his right hand, but the goats*
> *on the left. Then shall the King say unto them on his*
> *right hand, come, ye blessed of my Father, inherit the*
> *kingdom prepared for you from the foundation of the*
> *world.* (Matthew 25:31-34 KJV)

> *Then shall he say also unto them on the left hand,*
> *depart from me, ye cursed, into everlasting fire,*
> *prepared for the devil and his angels ... And these*
> *shall go away into everlasting punishment: but the*
> *righteous into life eternal.* (Matthew 25:41,46 KJV)

The people at the right hand of Christ were justified or declared righteous because of their faith in Christ. Their faith led them to act in a way that was pleasing to Christ and God. Those

who stood at the left hand of Christ were condemned because of
a lack of faith, and their works proved that they didn't know the
Lord. The separation that Christ brings is based upon faith in
Christ or lack of it:

> *But that no man is justified by the law in the sight*
> *of God, it is evident: for, the just shall live by faith.*
> (Galatians 3:11 KJV)[503]

The day will come when there will no longer be an opportunity
to believe in Christ and be saved. The truth will dawn on people
too late and they'll come knocking on the door of heaven asking
for entry. Christ will reject them, calling them workers of iniquity,
and saying that He doesn't know them. They will be thrust out
of heaven.[504]

Jesus promises His disciples that He will come back for them:

> *Let not your heart be troubled: ye believe in God,*
> *believe also in me. In my Father's house are many*
> *mansions: if it were not so, I would have told you. I*
> *go to prepare a place for you. And if I go and prepare*
> *a place for you, I will come again, and receive you*
> *unto myself; that where I am, there ye may be also.*
> (John 14:1-3 KJV)

Every disciple of Christ has this promise. Jesus warns every
believer to prepare for the day of His return because they don't
know when it will be. It will be a surprise to everyone. No one
knows when it will be, but God Himself:

---

[503] Habakkuk 2:4.
[504] Luke 13:24-28.

> *But of that day and hour knoweth no man, no, not the angels of heaven, but my Father only.* (Matthew 24:36 KJV)

Daniel prophesied that at sometime in the future, the kingdom of the Messiah would destroy all earthly kingdoms, and His kingdom would fill the earth and be established forever.[505] Daniel prophesied that there is a day of judgment awaiting at the time of the end of the world.[506] The Son of Man, the Messiah, will come and be given the kingdom.[507]

The prophecies in Daniel give a view of the coming of the Messiah and the inauguration of his kingdom. Jesus confirmed that he is the Messiah, the King of Israel, and the King of Creation. It will be the inauguration of the kingdom of Christ and God.

Part of preparing for the return of Christ is for every believer to confess Him before men. Once He's returned it's too late. Jesus promises His disciples that whoever confesses His name before men; Jesus will confess their names before God the Father.[508] True believers confess Christ now. But whoever is ashamed of Jesus, Jesus says that He will be ashamed of them before God the Father[509]. People who confess Christ and are not ashamed to claim Him as their own are promised a blessing by Christ, *"And blessed is he, whosoever shall not be offended in me."*[510] People who believe the testimony of Christ confess Him publicly before men. People who don't believe the testimony of Christ are ashamed of Him and offended by Him.

Jesus warned the disciples that many false prophets would

---

[505] Daniel 2:44.

[506] Daniel 7:9-10.

[507] Daniel 7:13-14.

[508] Matthew 10:32; Luke 12:8.

[509] Mark 8:38; Luke 9:26.

[510] Matthew 11:6 KJV.

come in His name, but they were not to believe them.[511] Jesus Himself is going to return in the glory of God with His holy angels, and He will reward every man according to his work.[512] He told the disciples that when He returns, it will be with power and great glory and His coming will illuminate the whole earth, in the same way as lightning flashes across the sky.[513] Anyone who claims to know the time of His return, or who claims he is Christ returned and calls on people to follow him is a liar.

Jesus promised that He would gather His disciples from every corner of the earth and Heaven. No one who has given his or her life to Christ would be left behind. Every person in Christ living on the earth, and every person in Christ who has died and gone to Heaven will be gathered to Him by the angels of God.[514]

---

[511] Matthew 24:4-5, 23-24; Mark 13:21-22.
[512] Matthew 16:27.
[513] Matthew 24:27; Luke 21:25-27.
[514] Mark 13:27.

7 Rejecting Eternal Life

As has been shown in all of the evidence that has been examined up until now, Jesus is the Christ, the Messiah, sent by God for the salvation of all mankind. He is the stone that the builders rejected, the foundation or cornerstone of life in God.[515]

The Apostle John calls Jesus the word of God and the light of men:

> In the beginning was the Word, and the Word was with God, and the Word was God. The same was in the beginning with God. All things were made by him; and without him was not any thing made that was made. In him was life; and the life was the light of men. And the light shineth in darkness; and the darkness comprehended it not. (John 1:1-5 KJV)

There is irrefutable evidence to the truth of Christ. If people have evidence, why do they reject Him? Why did Israel reject their Messiah? Why do people today reject Christ?

Jesus said why people would reject Him. The rejection of Christ by the Jews and the Romans in Jerusalem, and the rejection

---

[515] Matthew 21:42; Psalms 118:22-23.

of Christ by people today is because the light of Christ reveals their sin:

> And this is the condemnation, that light is come into the world, and men loved darkness rather than light, because their deeds were evil. For every one that doeth evil hateth the light, neither cometh to the light, lest his deeds should be reproved. (John 3:19-20 KJV)

God does not allow sin in His presence, it makes a separation between people and God; He becomes a stranger to them.[516] They don't know Christ and they don't know God:

> If I had not come and spoken unto them, they had not had sin: but now they have no cloke for their sin. He that hateth me hateth my Father also. If I had not done among them the works which none other man did, they had not had sin: but now have they both seen and hated both me and my Father. (John 15:22-24 KJV)

Jesus warned His disciples to be cautious concerning the leaven of the Pharisees and Sadducees, speaking of their doctrine.[517] What was the leaven of the Pharisees and the Sadducees? Both groups refused to believe that Jesus was the Christ, even when confronted by the overwhelming evidence of His many miracles and fulfillment of prophecy. Their doctrine was that no amount of evidence would ever cause them to submit to Jesus as the Messiah. They were unwilling to submit to the authority of Christ.

The same is true of people today, Jews and non-Jews alike, they refuse to believe in Jesus Christ no matter what evidence has

---

[516] Psalms 5:4-6; Isaiah 59:1-2.
[517] Matthew 16:6-12.

been presented to authenticate His message. Jesus warned that if people ignore God's word, even if someone came back from the dead, people wouldn't believe.[518]

The rulers of Israel and the rulers of Rome, the Jews and the Gentiles, rejected Christ when He came.[519] Peter quoted Psalm 2 where the word of God says the people plotted a vain thing to stand against the Lord. Something vain produces no result, it is useless, and has no hope of fulfillment. When people reject Christ, they reject God, and it is vain. Their rejection of God will not work out; it will not produce the result they hope for.

The people who were convicted by the preaching of John the Baptist repented, and upon repentance asked him what they should do to live in a way that was pleasing to God?[520] They understood that their previous lives were vain and wanted to change. Jesus said that in order to work the work of God they must believe in Him whom He sent.[521]

The leaders of the Jewish people rejected God's call to repentance given by John the Baptist, thinking they were righteous already and had no need of repentance or salvation.[522] They were the same as people today who say, "I'm a good person; I don't need forgiveness, and I don't need to be saved."

Jesus told the Pharisees and leaders of Israel that not only were they not righteous, but they were evil hypocrites, ignoring justice while pretending to pay letter-perfect attention to the law, making it impossible for other people to find God, oppressing the helpless, white-washed tombs full of dead men's bones, and lawless. Jesus pronounced them liars, hypocrites, unclean, blind guides, and

---

[518] Luke 16:31.
[519] Acts 4:25-28.
[520] Luke 3:10-14 KJV.
[521] John 6:29.
[522] Luke 7:29-30.

murderers.[523] Jesus says the same thing to anyone who thinks they can be good without God.

The Pharisees and Sadducees had turned from the worship of God to the worship of money.[524] They rejected Jesus because they didn't want to lose the wealth and benefits derived from their authority, position, and place in the life of Israel.[525]

In addition, the Jewish leaders rejected Jesus because He was not the conquering king who would free them from underneath the yoke of Roman rule. What good was a King of Israel who told them to submit to the Romans?[526]

Jesus told a parable to the Jewish leaders about a king who was going away to a far country to receive his kingdom. In the parable the people sent a delegation after him stating that they would not have this man to rule over them:

> *He said therefore, a certain nobleman went into a far country to receive for himself a kingdom, and to return. ... But his citizens hated him, and sent a message after him, saying, we will not have this man to reign over us. (Luke 19:12,14 KJV)*

Jesus told the Pharisees that when the king returned He was going to destroy all those who hated Him and refused to acknowledge his authority:

> *But those mine enemies, which would not that I should reign over them, bring hither, and slay them before me. (Luke 19:27 KJV)*

The Messiah has received a kingdom at the command of God.

---

[523] Matthew 23:13-35.

[524] Luke 16:13-15.

[525] John 11:47-48.

[526] Matthew 22:16-21.

All of those who reject Him, who hate Him, and who refuse to acknowledge His sovereignty, will be destroyed. God says that He will speak to all of those who hate the Messiah in His wrath, *"in His sore displeasure,"* and the Son of God will *"break them with a rod of iron."*[527]

People make excuses to ignore the call of God on their lives.[528] People reject Christ and follow after their own desires. Everything in their lives is more important than Christ and God, their families, their work, and their pursuits.[529] They think their lives here on earth, their positions, and their possessions mean more to them than anything God has to offer. *The Bible* says they are deceived.[530]

In addition to all of the reasons previously enumerated, people reject Christ because the sacrifice of Christ and the word of God is foolishness to them. *The Bible* tells us that the things of God are spiritually discerned.[531] People don't believe that *The Bible* is the word of God and the truth, so they ignore it. They think that if God exists, He is a loving God who won't condemn anyone to eternal punishment. They think that if there is an eternal afterlife, everyone will be there, and there is no need to change their lives. They dismiss the demands of Christ and the word of God thinking they can be ignored without penalty.

The testimony of Christ is the truth. If people know the truth but reject it, they are clinging to fantasies. They're clinging to dreams of finding fulfillment in their life on this earth. They have desires to be rich and possess things, or to be beautiful, or to be powerful, or to be wise. Their desire is to exalt themselves over others.

They must ignore the word of God and the testimony of Christ

---

[527] Psalms 2.
[528] Luke 14:16-24.
[529] Luke 14:18-20.
[530] Romans 7:11, Galatians 6:7, 2 Timothy 3:13, Titus 3:3.
[531] 1 Corinthians 1:23, 1 Corinthians 2:14.

in order to chase after these dreams. A man or woman without Christ is a man or woman without God.[532] They allow their dreams and their fantasies to corrupt them. They are like Satan.

Isaiah told us of Satan's desires:

> *For thou hast said in thine heart, I will ascend into heaven, I will exalt my throne above the stars of God: I will sit also upon the mount of the congregation, in the sides of the north: I will ascend above the heights of the clouds; I will be like the most High.* (Isaiah 14:13-14 KJV)

Satan's pride caused him to desire to exalt himself because of his wisdom and his beauty. He told himself that he was worthy of being like God, even though he is a creation of God and has none of the attributes of the Creator. God created Satan and never will any creature be exalted above his creator. God revealed to Ezekiel that the Satan corrupted his wisdom because of his beauty:

> *Thine heart was lifted up because of thy beauty, thou hast corrupted thy wisdom by reason of thy brightness: I will cast thee to the ground, I will lay thee before kings, that they may behold thee.* (Ezekiel 28:17 KJV)

Peter tempted Jesus to ignore the will of God and to take another road besides death on the cross when he told him he didn't have to die:

> *From that time forth began Jesus to shew unto his disciples, how that he must go unto Jerusalem, and suffer many things of the elders and chief priests and scribes, and be killed, and be raised again the third*

---

[532] 1 John 2:22-23.

day. Then Peter took him, and began to rebuke him,
saying, be it far from thee, Lord: this shall not be unto
thee. (Matthew 16:21-22 KJV)

But Jesus Christ rebuked Peter, calling him Satan, and condemned Satan and men for ignoring the things of God, saying that Satan and men had the same desires:

But he turned, and said unto Peter, get thee behind
me, Satan: thou art an offence unto me: for thou
savourest not the things that be of God, but those that
be of men. (Matthew 16:23 KJV)

The desires of Satan and of men cause them to turn their backs to God and exalt themselves. When they ignore the truth to chase their dreams they sin against their own souls and all they have to look forward to is judgment:

For if we sin wilfully after that we have received the
knowledge of the truth, there remaineth no more
sacrifice for sins, but a certain fearful looking for of
judgment and fiery indignation, which shall devour
the adversaries. (Hebrews 10:26-27 KJV)

Jesus told the parable of the kingdom of heaven about the man invited to the wedding of the king who refused to wear the wedding garment provided by the king:

And when the king came in to see the guests, he saw
there a man which had not on a wedding garment:
and he saith unto him, friend, how camest thou in
hither not having a wedding garment? And he was
speechless. Then said the king to the servants, bind
him hand and foot, and take him away, and cast

> *him into outer darkness; there shall be weeping and*
> *gnashing of teeth. For many are called, but few are*
> *chosen.* (Matthew 22:11-14 KJV)

God provides the wedding garment, and it is the righteousness of Christ. It was purchased with his blood on the cross.[533] It is the garment of salvation.[534] God clothes us in Christ. God invites people to heaven, to the wedding of the King. Christ is the bridegroom and the saints are his bride. But they must make use of the way He has provided.

All those who reject Christ and try to stand in their own righteousness are rejecting the wedding garment that God has given to cover them, and they stand naked before God.[535] Whoever refuses to wear the robe of righteousness that God has provided will be cast out into outer darkness where there will be weeping and wailing. It will be an everlasting torment.[536]

Jesus promises us that at the end of the world God is going to send forth His angels and separate the wicked from the just:

> *So shall it be at the end of the world: the angels shall*
> *come forth, and sever the wicked from among the*
> *just, and shall cast them into the furnace of fire: there*
> *shall be wailing and gnashing of teeth.* (Matthew
> 13:49-50 KJV)

God promises a day of judgment for every person who doesn't know Christ. All who refuse to accept Christ refuse to allow their names to be written in the *Lamb's Book of Life*. They will be judged on their own merits, on their own righteousness, and *The Bible* tells us that they will be condemned to an everlasting destruction:

---

[533] Revelation 6:11, 7:9-14.
[534] Isaiah 61:10
[535] Hebrews 4:13.
[536] Matthew 25:41,46.

> *And I saw a great white throne, and him that sat
> on it, from whose face the earth and the heaven fled
> away; and there was found no place for them. And
> I saw the dead, small and great, stand before God;
> and the books were opened: and another book was
> opened, which is the book of life: and the dead were
> judged out of those things which were written in the
> books, according to their works. And the sea gave up
> the dead which were in it; and death and hell delivered
> up the dead which were in them: and they were judged
> every man according to their works. And death and
> hell were cast into the lake of fire. This is the second
> death. And whosoever was not found written in the
> book of life was cast into the lake of fire.* (Revelation
> 20:11-15 KJV)

Is God evil because he casts people into the Lake of Fire forever because of sin? It is God's righteousness that demands a penalty for sin. God offers salvation to anyone who will repent and believe in Christ. If people willingly refuse the offer of a gracious God to save them, it is not God condemning them but they themselves, and God accedes to their will. God's desire is for everyone to be saved, but He will not force anyone to accept His salvation.

God told the house of Israel to get a new heart and a new spirit, because the heart and spirit that they had was leading them to death:

> *Cast away from you all your transgressions, whereby
> ye have transgressed; and make you a new heart and
> a new spirit: for why will ye die, O house of Israel?
> For I have no pleasure in the death of him that dieth,
> saith the Lord God: wherefore turn yourselves, and
> live ye.* (Ezekiel 18:31-32 KJV)

God says the same thing to people today, "*Why will you die?*" God doesn't take pleasure in the punishment or death of the wicked. God says that no one should take pleasure in the misfortune or punishment of others.[537] The punishment of God is meant to correct sin, and death is meant to end the sin that won't be corrected. God says that He doesn't take pleasure in the death of the wicked:

> *Therefore, O thou son of man, speak unto the house of Israel; thus ye speak, saying, if our transgressions and our sins be upon us, and we pine away in them, how should we then live? Say unto them, as I live, saith the Lord God, I have no pleasure in the death of the wicked; but that the wicked turn from his way and live: turn ye, turn ye from your evil ways; for why will ye die, O house of Israel?* (Ezekiel 33:10-11 KJV)

God has shown His heart and His love for men and women by sacrificing His Son on the cross that they might live.[538] Find the heart of God in Christ on the cross.

When we refuse to believe that Jesus is the Christ, who is the only way for us to be saved, we turn our backs on God, and we walk down into the darkness.[539]

Peter tells us that God is delaying His judgment so that men and women can be saved:

> *The Lord is not slack concerning His promise, as some count slackness, but is longsuffering toward us, not willing that any should perish but that all should come to repentance.* (2 Peter 3:9 NKJV)

---

[537] Proverbs 24:17-18.
[538] Romans 5:8.
[539] Proverbs 15:24, 4:18.

The corroboration of the testimony of Christ has been given to us so that we might believe the truth of Christ and have eternal life:

> *And truly Jesus did many other signs in the presence of His disciples, which are not written in this book; but these are written that you may believe that Jesus is the Christ, the Son of God, and that believing you may have life in His name.* (John 20:30-31 NKJV)

8 The Moment of Truth

Well, anyone who has gotten this far in this book and hasn't given their life to Christ should take a moment and reflect about the truth of Christ that has been revealed. It's time to take action to ensure that your life is hid with Christ in God. God is calling you to eternal life. Will you ignore it, or will you accept God's gift of Christ?

There is nothing complicated about asking God to forgive you and make you his son or daughter. You only need to repent and acknowledge the truth of God's word, that you are a sinner headed for destruction before a holy God and need the salvation that is only found in Christ. Pray right now to God. Tell Him that you're sorry for your sin and rebellion towards Him and want to be forgiven and saved. Pray this prayer to God:

"Father everything your word says is true, I've sinned and I need your forgiveness. I know that Jesus Christ is your Son and that you sent Him to die on the cross for me, to take the punishment that my sins deserve. I believe that you raised Jesus from the dead that I might be justified.[540] Lord Jesus, please come to live in my heart, forgive me and cleanse me from my sin, and be my Lord."

The moment that you pray this and believe it, you are forgiven, you are born again, and you have eternal life. It's not something

---

[540] Romans 8:33.

that you wait for. *The Bible* promises that you're saved the moment you repent and believe in Jesus Christ as your Lord.[541]

You've been born again. Maybe you feel different and maybe you don't. The life of a Christian is a life of faith, faith in God and in His word. Your life is not based on how you feel, but on what God says about you, on what God has promised.[542] God cannot lie.[543] You are now a son or daughter of the living God.[544]

There are three phases in the life of every Christian, justification, sanctification, and glorification. You've taken the first step, asking for the forgiveness of God and eternal life in Christ. This is what allows God to justify you. The moment you are born again, you are justified. You are no longer condemned:

> *There is therefore now no condemnation to them which are in Christ Jesus, who walk not after the flesh, but after the Spirit.* (Romans 8:1 NKJV)

Believers are not saved or justified by anything that they do. God justifies them strictly on the basis of the work of Christ on the cross, there is nothing that they can ever do to merit or earn their salvation; it is a free gift from God.[545]

The second phase of the Christian life is called sanctification. Sanctification is the process by which God separates believers from the world and everything that is contrary to the truth and the holiness of God and draws them close to Him. Sanctification is accomplished in believer's lives when they are obedient to the word of Christ and yield to the Holy Spirit who is now residing

---

[541] Romans 10:9-10,13.

[542] 2 Corinthians 5:7.

[543] Titus 1:2.

[544] John 1:12-13.

[545] Ephesians 2:8-9.

in them.[546] *The Bible* says that as sons and daughters of God they must cleanse themselves of everything He hates.[547]

The rest of a believer's life on this earth is a battle between the new life in Christ and the old life in the flesh. God commands all of His children to walk in the Spirit:

> *I say then: walk in the Spirit, and you shall not fulfill the lust of the flesh. For the flesh lusts against the Spirit, and the Spirit against the flesh; and these are contrary to one another, so that you do not do the things that you wish.* (Galatians 5:16-17 NKJV)

Believers are in a battle to allow the Holy Spirit of God to sanctify them. They are sanctified by the work of the Holy Spirit through the word of God. Speaking of Christ and the believers who make up the church, Paul says that Christ cleanses them by washing them in the water of the word so that they might be pure and clean.[548]

The Holy Spirit can only use the word of God to sanctify someone if they are studying it. Everyone who is born again has a desire to know God and His word. Participate in the work of sanctification by the Holy Spirit by reading God's word everyday. Set aside a time that is God's alone and read His word. Pray to God to give understanding and wisdom in His word. It is only by the enlightenment of the Holy Spirit that someone can understand the word of God.[549] Everyone should start by reading the New Testament all the way through. Don't worry about how long it takes. Read one or two chapters everyday and let God use His word to cleanse you and change you. He will show you new things every time you read His word. Whenever you read the word of God

---

[546] 1 Corinthians 3:16.

[547] 2 Corinthians 7:1.

[548] Ephesians 5:26-27.

[549] 1 Corinthians 2:12-14.

and He shows you something, humble yourself before God and be obedient to His word.

Victory in the battle for sanctification comes because believers submit themselves to God and His word. Knowing the word of God, they resist everything contrary to godliness, all of the temptations and lies of Satan.[550]

Their sanctification also occurs by being around other Christians who are walking in love towards God and each other. Believers need to belong to a local church where they can grow in Christ. When they assemble with other Christians to worship the Lord and hear His word, they help encourage each other to be obedient to the Lord and His commands:

> *And let us consider one another to provoke unto love and to good works: not forsaking the assembling of ourselves together, as the manner of some is; but exhorting one another: and so much the more, as ye see the day approaching.* (Hebrews 10:24-25 KJV)

Find a church that believes that *The Bible* is the word of God, and preaches and lives by it. Find people who are walking in the truth and love of Christ and follow their example.[551] Pray to God to help you find a church that is worshipping Him in spirit and truth.[552] God will lead you to a faithful church if you ask Him to.

The Bible tells us that it is only by faith that someone can please God:

> *But without faith it is impossible to please him: for he that cometh to God must believe that he is, and*

---

[550] James 4:7-8.
[551] 1 Corinthians 11:1.
[552] John 4:24.

that he is a rewarder of them that diligently seek him.
(Hebrews 11:6 KJV)

Faith to believe in Christ is a gift of God whenever someone is born again. Once they've been born again and have the Holy Spirit living in them, the fruit of the Holy Spirit is faith.[553] They increase their faith by studying the word of God.[554] Faith means ignoring how one feels and the wisdom of the world. A believer's faith is founded on the truth of God and Christ. It is a faith in God alone, and believers trust Him to do everything that He's promised.

When anyone becomes a Christian, God gives him or her a love for Him, a love for Christ, and a love for the truth. Jesus said that the word of God is the truth, and He prayed that God would sanctify every believer by His word.[555] Everything that the believer does is based on the truth that God has revealed in His word. The people who refuse to give their lives to Christ perish because they haven't received a love for the truth.[556]

Believers give their lives to Christ in gratitude for His forgiveness and salvation. Forever after they are in a personal relationship with God, the God who created everyone, and the God who died to save them. That personal relationship with God is manifested by His Holy Spirit living in the believer. Jesus called the Holy Spirit, *"The Comforter,"* and said He would live in every son and daughter of God forever; God would not leave them orphans:

> *If ye love me, keep my commandments. And I will pray the Father, and he shall give you another Comforter, that he may abide with you for ever; even*

---

[553] Galatians 5:22-23.
[554] Romans 10:17.
[555] John 17:17.
[556] 2 Thessalonians 2:9-12.

> *the Spirit of truth; whom the world cannot receive,*
> *because it seeth him not, neither knoweth him: but ye*
> *know him; for he dwelleth with you, and shall be in*
> *you. I will not leave you comfortless [NKJV:orphans]:*
> *I will come to you.* (John 14:15-18 KJV)

Christians are in a personal relationship with God. It is indescribable what it means to go to God everyday in prayer and have Him pour out His love and truth in their lives, to know the joy that comes when they worship Him for who He is and what He's done. Once they know God and have His Holy Spirit dwelling in them it becomes hard to understand how other people can live without Him. When Christians are faithful to their confession of faith in Christ, day-by-day they come to know more and more the comfort of the Holy Spirit.

> *Peace I leave with you, my peace I give unto you:*
> *not as the world giveth, give I unto you. Let not*
> *your heart be troubled, neither let it be afraid.* (John
> 14:27 KJV)

The final phase of the Christian life is glorification. Christians are looking forward to the day when God reveals the glory of Christ in them.[557] God is going to bring them to glory. He is able to keep them from stumbling and falling in their walk with Christ. They will be made perfect at the time of God's choosing. They are waiting for their perfection in Christ, their promised glorification:

> *Now unto him that is able to keep you from falling,*
> *and to present you faultless before the presence of his*
> *glory with exceeding joy, to the only wise God our*

---

[557] Romans 8:18.

Saviour, be glory and majesty, dominion and power,
both now and ever. Amen. (Jude 1:24-25 KJV)

At the time of Christ's return, whether a Christian has died and gone to heaven, or he is still alive on the earth, God is going to give him a new, perfect, resurrection body, the same as Christ has.[558] In an instant every Christian will be changed:

> *Behold, I shew you a mystery; we shall not all sleep,*
> *but we shall all be changed, in a moment, in the*
> *twinkling of an eye, at the last trump: for the trumpet*
> *shall sound, and the dead shall be raised incorruptible,*
> *and we shall be changed. For this corruptible must*
> *put on incorruption, and this mortal must put on*
> *immortality.* (1 Corinthians 15:51-53 NKJV)

> *For the Lord himself shall descend from heaven with*
> *a shout, with the voice of the archangel, and with the*
> *trump of God: and the dead in Christ shall rise first:*
> *then we which are alive and remain shall be caught*
> *up together with them in the clouds, to meet the Lord*
> *in the air: and so shall we ever be with the Lord.* (1
> Thessalonians 4:16-17 NKJV)

The Bible says that in the presence of God is fullness of joy.[559] Let the joy that comes from your salvation rise up to God in thanksgiving to Him for what He's done in you:

> *But I have trusted in thy mercy; my heart shall rejoice*
> *in thy salvation. I will sing unto the Lord, because he*
> *hath dealt bountifully with me.* (Psalms 13:5-6 KJV)

---

[558] Luke 24:39; 1 John 3:1-3.
[559] Psalms 16:11.

Jesus has revealed the heart of God. He is the true and faithful witness, the firstborn from the dead, and the King of Creation.[560] By His own blood He has broken the power of sin in the lives of every Christian and redeemed them to God the Father so that they can be with Him forever. Every Christian is waiting expectantly for his return:

> *"Behold, I am coming quickly! Blessed is he who keeps the words of the prophecy of this book." ... He who testifies to these things says, "Surely I am coming quickly." Amen. Even so, come, Lord Jesus! The grace of our Lord Jesus Christ be with you all. Amen.* (Revelation 22:7, 20-21 NKJV)

---

[560] Revelation 1:5-7

9 How to Reach the Author

Stephen W. Lange is available for book readings and signings, panel discussions, and as a guest lecturer, upon request. U.S. trade bookstores and wholesalers please contact:

Stephen W. Lange
21346 Saint Andrews Boulevard, #139
Boca Raton, FL 33433
steve.lange@ContendingForChrist.org
1-561-325-7525
https://www.ContendingForChrist.org

Special discounts available on quantity purchases.

Steve is also the author of "Contending For Christ," a book about the spiritual warfare that every Christian faces trying to live a godly life in an ungodly world.

Both titles are available on Amazon in print and Kindle electronic formats.

Follow Steve's blog: *https://www.DeliverMyFeet.org*

10 Appendix

10.1 The Reliability of The Bible

Here is a partial list of writers and resources confirming the reliability of *The Bible*:

1. Christian Apologetics and Research Ministry: *https://carm. org/bible*

2. Focus on the Family: *http://www.focusonthefamily.com/ faith/the-study-of-god/how-do-we-know-the-bible-is-true/ is-the-bible-reliable*

3. Tim Keller: *https://evidencetobelieve.net/reliability-of-the-bible/*

4. *From God to Us: How we got our Bible.* Copyright © 1974 by Norman L. Geisler and William Nix. Chicago: Moody Press

5. *Are the New Testament Documents Reliable?* Copyright © 1943 by F. F. Bruce.

6. *God Breathed.* Copyright © 2015 by Josh McDowell Ministry.

7. *I Don't Have Enough Faith to be an Atheist.* Copyright © 2004 by Norman L. Geisler and Frank Turek.

10.2 Proof of the Resurrection of Christ

Here is a list of some of the writers who have reported on the truth of the resurrection of Christ:

1. *The Case for Christ*, by Lee Strobel. Copyright © 1998. Published by Zondervan, Grand Rapids, Michigan. 49530.
2. *Evidence That Demands a Verdict*, by Josh McDowell. Copyright © 1972, 1979, Campus Crusade for Christ, Inc. Here's Life Publishers, Inc., P.O. Box 1576, San Bernardino, CA 92402.
3. *I Don't Have Enough Faith to Be an Atheist*, by Normal L. Geisler and Frank Turek. Copyright © 2004. Published by Crossway Books, a division of Good News Publishers, 1300 Crescent Street, Wheaton, Illinois 60187.

Printed in the United States
By Bookmasters